50 step by steps

HAIR'S HOW ®

Content / Table des matières / Inhalt / Contenido

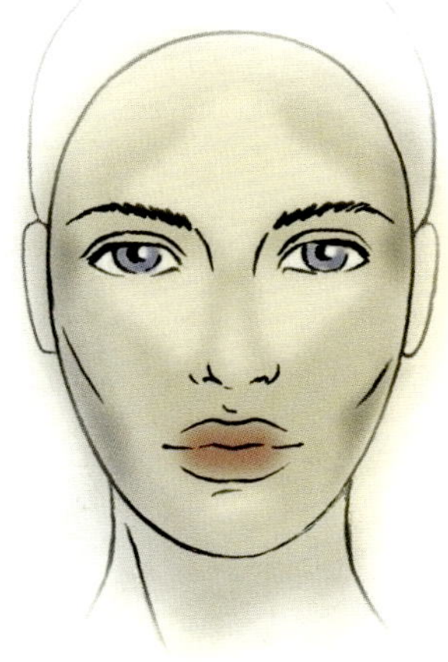

1. Oval face / Visage ovale
Ovale Gesichtsform / Cara ovalada

FACE

The basis of any makeup is a light and shade correction of the face that will help to soften too sharp lines and make too soft lines more expressive. For this you will need light and dark concealers. Powder, blusher, and even natural palette shadow will do, too.

LE VISAGE

La base de tout maquillage est un travail sur le jeu des ombres et des lumières du visage, qui permet d'adoucir les angles trop saillants ou d'ajouter plus d'expressivité aux contours trop flous. Pour cela nous allons avoir besoin de correcteurs foncés et clairs. La poudre, les fards à joues et même les ombres à paupières aux tons naturels peuvent également nous servir à cela.

GESICHT

Die Basis eines jeden Make-ups ist eine Licht- und Schattenkorrektur des Gesichts, um harte Konturen weicher zu machen und weicheren Konturen mehr Ausdruck zu verleihen. Hierzu benötigen Sie helle und dunkle Concealer, Puder, Rouge, aber auch eine Palette natürlicher Lidschattenfarben ist ausreichend.

CARA

La base del maquillaje es corregir el tono y el brillo de la cara, de manera que ayuden a suavizar las líneas muy pronunciadas y, también, a hacer que las líneas demasiado suaves sean más expresivas. Para esto es necesario contar con correctores claros y oscuros. Polvo, rubor y también una paleta de sombras de color natural.

1. If your face shape is close to oval, you are lucky – it is considered to be an ideal one. All you need is to mask small problems of your skin with a concealer.
2. A long face should be visually «shortened and widened". For this, apply the dark concealer along the hair line and the chin line, and also to the area under the cheekbones smudging it by horizontal lines towards the alae of the nose.
3. A round face should be visually "narrowed". Do the following: apply the darker concealer to the lateral parts of the forehead and under the cheekbones directing diagonal lines towards the lip corners. Apply the light concealer to the T-zone.
4. A square face needs softening, so apply the dark concealer to the most protuberant parts of the face, distribute light tone over the center of the face.
5. A rectangular face is extended and angu-

1. Si votre visage est proche de la forme ovale, vous avez de la chance, puisque cette forme est considérée comme étant idéale. Il ne vous reste donc qu'à camoufler les discrètes imperfections de la peau à l'aide d'un correcteur.
2. Un visage allongé peut être visuellement raccourci et élargi. Pour ce faire, appliquez un correcteur sombre en suivant le contour du visage le long de la racine des cheveux et des maxillaires (mâchoires), ainsi qu'en-dessous des pommettes, en l'estompant avec un geste horizontal vers les narines.
3. Vous pouvez rendre un visage rond visuellement plus étroit. Procédez de cette manière : appliquez un correcteur plus foncé sur les côtés du visage et en-dessous des pommettes en allant en diagonale vers les commissures des lèvres. Utilisez un correcteur clair pour la zone en « T ».
4. Pour arrondir un visage carré il faut

1. Entspricht Ihr Gesicht ungefähr einer ovalen Gesichtsform, können Sie sich glücklich schätzen – oval ist die ideale Gesichtsform. Sie müssen lediglich kleine Unregelmäßigkeiten Ihrer Haut mit einem Concealer abdecken.
2. Eine längliche Gesichtsform sollte optisch „verkürzt und breiter" gemacht werden. Hierzu tragen Sie den dunklen Concealer am Haaransatz, entlangder Kinnlinie und unterhalb der Wangenknochen auf, um diesen dann horizontal zu den Nasenflügeln hin zu verwischen.
3. Eine runde Gesichtsform sollte optisch „verschmälert" werden. Tragen Sie den dunklen Concealer auf die seitlichen Stirnpartien und unterhalb der Wangenknochen, diagonal zu den Mundwinkeln hin, auf. Tragen Sie den hellen Concealer auf die T-Zone auf.
4. Eine quadratische Gesichtsform muss

1. Si la forma de tu cara es semejante a un óvalo, entonces eres afortunado – se la considera la ideal. Lo único que necesitas es ocultar los pequeños problemas de piel con un corrector.
2. Una cara alargada debe ser visualmente «acortada y ensanchada». Para esto, aplicar un corrector oscuro a lo largo de la línea del pelo y en la línea de la pera y, también en el área debajo de los pómulos, esfumándolo mediante líneas horizontales hacia las alas de la nariz.
3. Una cara redonda debe ser visualmente "angostada". Haga lo siguiente: aplique el corrector oscuro a ambos lados de la frente y debajo de los pómulos trazando líneas diagonales hacia la comisura de los labios. Aplique el corrector claro en la zona de la T.
4. La cara cuadrada necesita ser suavizada, entonces aplicar el corrector oscu-

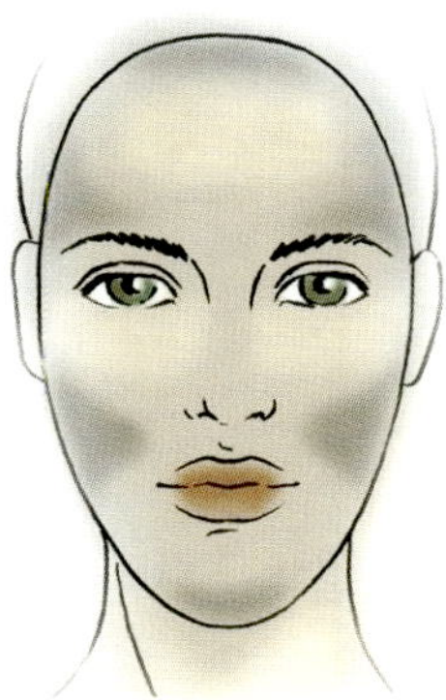

2. Long face / Visage allongé
Längliche Gesichtsform / Cara alargada

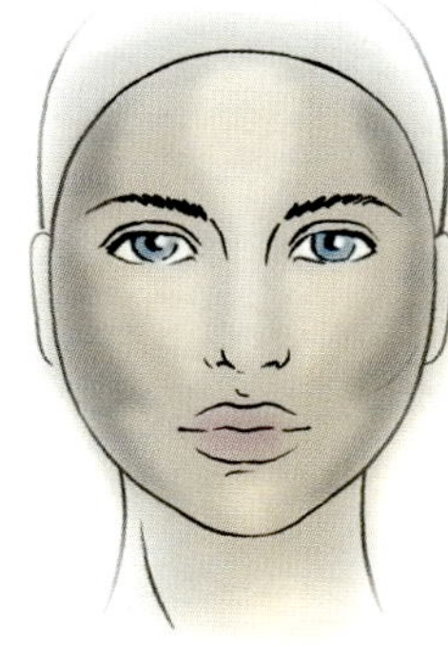

3. Round face / Visage rond
Runde Gesichtsform / Cara redonda

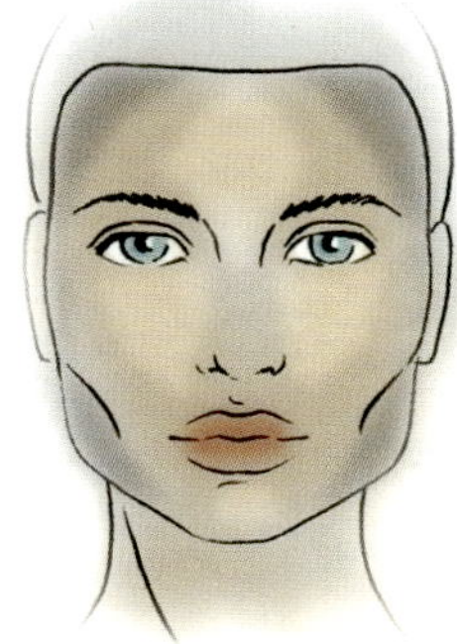

4. Square face / Visage carré
Quadratische Gesichtsform / Cara cuadrada

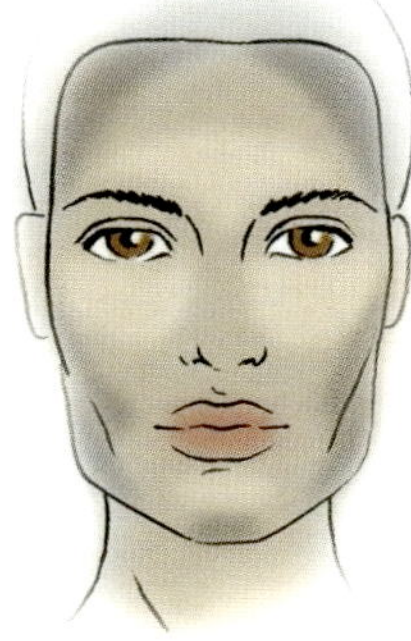

5. Rectangular face / Visage rectangulaire
Rechteckige Gesichtsform / Cara rectangular

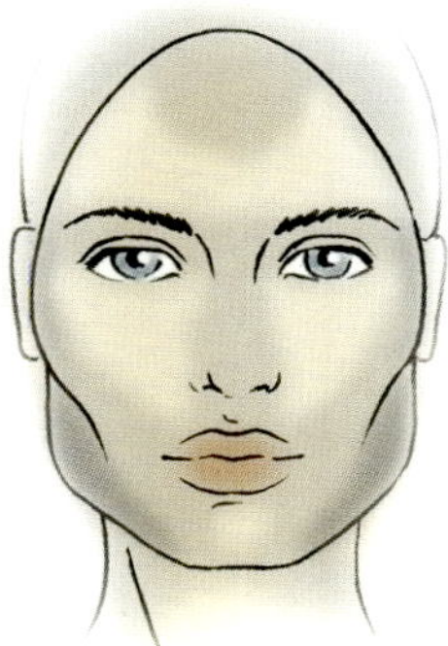

6. Trapezium-shaped face / Visage en triangle haut / Trapezförmige Gesichtsform / Cara trapezoidal

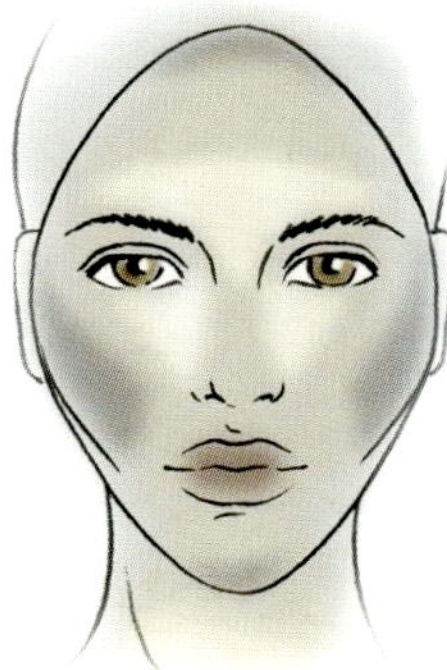

7. Diamond-shaped face / Visage hexagonal
Diamantförmige Gesichtsform / Cara con forma de diamante

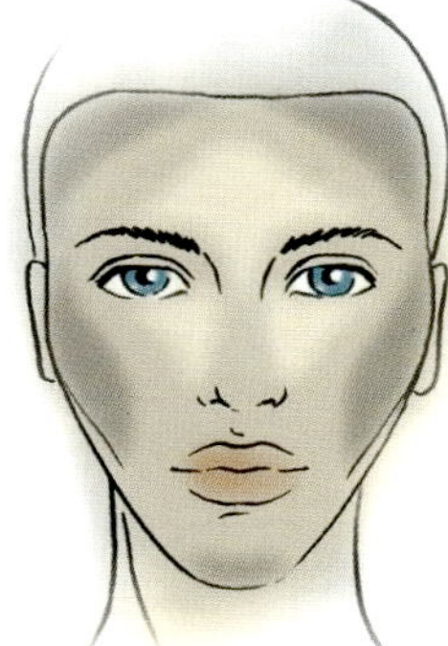

8. Triangular face / Visage en triangle bas
Dreieckige Gesichtsform / Cara triangular

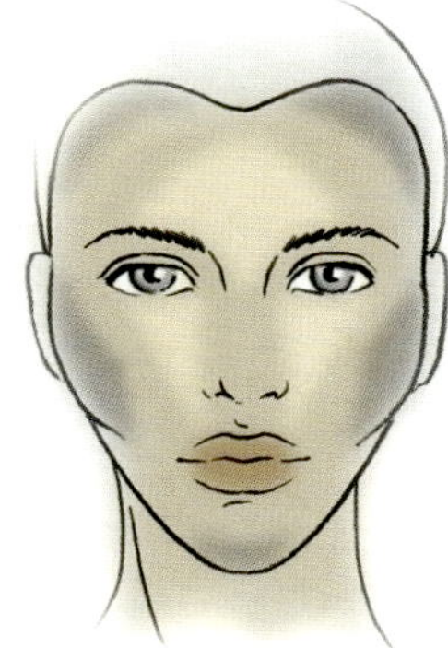

9. Heartlet face / Visage en cœur
Herzförmige Gesichtsform / Cara acorazonada

lar, that is why you will have to "narrow" and "widen" it at the same time. First apply the dark concealer to the most protuberant parts of the face and to the chin, then smudge it under the cheekbones horizontally towards the alae of the nose.

6. A trapezium-shaped (pear-shaped) face is a face with a narrow forehead and wide chin. Apply the darker concealer to the wide part of the face that will narrow it visually, to the forehead – the light concealer to make it wider; thus, the forehead and chin will be counterbalanced.

7. A diamond-shape face looks angular, so it should be softened. Apply the darker concealer to the sharp, protuberant cheekbones, and also along the hair line and to the chin smudging it horizontally.

8. A triangular face needs softening, too: apply the dark concealer to the wide angular parts of the forehead, protuberant sharp cheekbones and chin. Accentuate the central part of the face with the lighter concealer.

9. A heartlet face resembles a triangular one, that is why when correcting it act in the similar way: soften the prominent parts of the forehead and sharp chin with the dark concealer, while applying the light one to the central part of the face.

appliquer un correcteur foncé sur les angles les plus saillants et répartir du correcteur clair sur le centre du visage.

5. Un visage rectangulaire est long et anguleux, donc il faut le raccourcir et l'élargir en même temps. Appliquez d'abord le correcteur sur les angles les plus saillants et sur le menton, et ensuite estompez-le sous les pommettes en allant à l'horizontale vers les narines.

6. Un visage hexagonal (en forme de poire) est un visage au front étroit et au menton large. Étendez du correcteur foncé sur la partie large du visage, ce qui le rendra visuellement plus étroit, et du correcteur clair sur le front qui paraîtra plus large, de cette manière le front et le menton seront plus harmonieux.

7. Un visage en triangle haut est un visage anguleux, il faut donc l'adoucir. Appliquez du correcteur foncé sur les pommettes saillantes et pointues et tout le long des racines des cheveux et sur le menton, étendez-le à l'horizontale.

8. Pour adoucir un visage en triangle bas, appliquez le correcteur foncé sur les parties larges et anguleuses du menton, sur les pommettes saillantes et le menton. Eclaircissez la partie médiane du visage.

9. Un visage en cœur ressemble à un visage en triangle bas, c'est pourquoi il faut le corriger de la même façon : utilisez le correcteur foncé pour adoucir les parties saillantes du front et le menton pointu, réservez le correcteur clair pour le milieu du visage.

weicher gestaltet werden. Tragen Sie hierzu den dunklen Concealer auf die Stellen des Gesichts auf, die am stärksten hervortreten. Verteilen Sie den helleren Ton über die Gesichtsmitte.

5. Eine rechteckige Gesichtsform ist lang und kantig und muss „verschmälert" und gleichzeitig „verbreitert" werden. Tragen Sie zuerst den dunklen Concealer auf das Kinn und die Stellen des Gesichts auf, die am stärksten hervortreten. Verwischen Sie diesen nun unterhalb der Wangenknochen, horizontal zu den Nasenflügeln hin.

6. Eine trapezförmige Gesichtsform (birnenförmig) zeichnet sich durch eine schmale Stirnpartie und ein breites Kinn aus. Tragen Sie den dunkleren Concealer auf den breiten Teil des Gesichts auf, um diesen optisch zu verschmälern. Die Stirnpartie wird durch den helleren Concealer optisch erweitert. Somit wird ein Ausgleich zwischen Stirn und Kinn geschaffen.

7. Eine diamantenförmige Gesichtsform ist eckig und muss somit „weicher" gemacht werden. Tragen Sie den dunkleren Concealer auf die hart-wirkenden, hervortretenden Wangenknochen, entlang des Haaransatzes und auf das Kinn auf und verwischen Sie diesen horizontal.

8. Eine dreieckigeGesichtsform muss ebenfalls „weicher" gemacht werden. Tragen Sie den dunklen Concealer auf die breiten, kantigen Konturen der Stirnpartie, hervortretenden, hohen Wangenknochen und das Kinn auf. Betonen Sie die Gesichtsmitte mit dem helleren Concealer.

9. Eine herzförmige Gesichtsform ähnelt einer dreieckigen Gesichtsform. Von daher ist die Korrektur ähnlich: Enthärten Sie die hervortretende Stirnpartie und das spitze Kinn mit einem dunklen Concealer und tragen Sie den hellen Concealer auf die Mitte des Gesichts auf.

ro a las zonas más protuberantes de la cara, distribuir corrector claro en el centro de la cara.

5. Una cara rectangular es alargada y angulosa, es por eso, que hay que afinar y ensanchar al mismo tiempo. Primero, aplicar el corrector oscuro a las partes más protuberantes de la cara y en la pera, luego, esfumarlo bajo los pómulos horizontalmente hacia las alas de la nariz.

6. Una cara de forma trapezoidal (forma de pera) es una cara que tiene una frente angosta y una pera ancha. Aplicar el corrector oscuro a la parte ancha para angostarla visualmente, en la frente – el corrector claro para ensancharla; de este modo, la pera y la frente estarán equilibradas.

7. Una cara con forma de diamante luce angulosa, por lo que necesita ser suavizada. Aplicar el corrector más oscuro sobre los angulares y protuberantes pómulos y, también, a lo largo de la línea del pelo y la pera, esfumándolo de manera horizontal.

8. Una cara triangular también necesita ser suavizada: aplicar el corrector oscuro sobre las partes anchas de la frente, las protuberancias de los pómulos y pera. Acentuar la parte central de la cara con el corrector más claro.

9. Una cara acorazonada semeja la triangular, por lo que al corregirla hay que proceder de manera similar: suavizar las partes prominentes de la frente, y la pera afilada con un corrector oscuro. En tanto que, aplicar el corrector claro sobre el centro de la cara.

EYES

Makeup with a focus on the eyes is always relevant, both for creating a casual image and for going out. Shadow is, beyond all doubt, the main means to "make the eyes more expressive". It will not only accentuate the color of the iris, but also help to correct the eye shape.

LES YEUX

Le maquillage qui fait ressortir les yeux est toujours d'actualité, autant pour un look quotidien que pour une grande occasion. Le fard à paupières est le moyen principal utilisé pour intensifier le regard. Les fards à paupières ne font pas seulement ressortir la couleur de l'iris, mais aussi permettent de corriger la forme des yeux.

AUGEN

Make-up mit Fokus auf die Augen ist immer relevant – sowohl für den Alltag als auch am Abend. Lidschatten ist zweifellos das Nonplusultra, um „Augen Ausdruck zu verleihen". Er betont nicht nur die Augenfarbe sondern kann auch zur Korrektur der Augenform verwendet werden.

OJOS

Siempre es importante centrar el maquillaje en los ojos, tanto para crear un estilo casual, como para una salida. La sombra es, sin lugar a dudas, el mejor medio para "lograr ojos más expresivos". No solo acentúan el color del iris, sino que también ayudan a corregir la forma de los ojos.

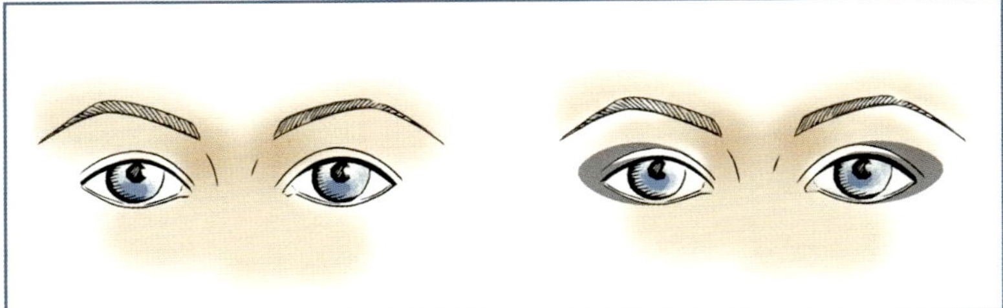

The classic shape of eyes is close to the ideal one. To accentuate it, highlight the outer eye corner with shadow that will suit the color of the iris. And remember the basic rule: dark shadow should be applied to the outer eye corner, the light one – to the movable lid and under the eyebrows.

La forme classique des yeux est proche de l'idéal. Pour les mettre en valeur, travaillez le coin extérieur de l'œil avec des fards à paupières correspondant à la couleur de l'iris. Et retenez cette règle fondamentale : les fards à paupières sombres sont appliqués sur le coin extérieur de l'œil, tandis que ceux qui sont clairs sont appliqués sur la paupière mobile et sur l'arcade sourcilière.

Eine klassische Augenform ist perfekt. Um diese zu betonen, heben Sie den äußeren Augenwinkel mit einem Lidschatten hervor, der Ihrer Augenfarbe schmeichelt. Denken Sie an die Faustregel: Dunkler Lidschatten sollte auf den äußeren Augenwinkel und heller Lidschatten auf das bewegliche Augenlid und unterhalb der Augenbrauen aufgetragen werden.

La forma clásica de los ojos. Cercana a la forma ideal. Para acentuarla, resaltar el borde externo con una sombra que combine con el color del iris. Recuerde una regla básica: la sombra más oscura debe aplicarse el borde externo del ojo, la más clara, sobre el párpado móvil y bajo las cejas.

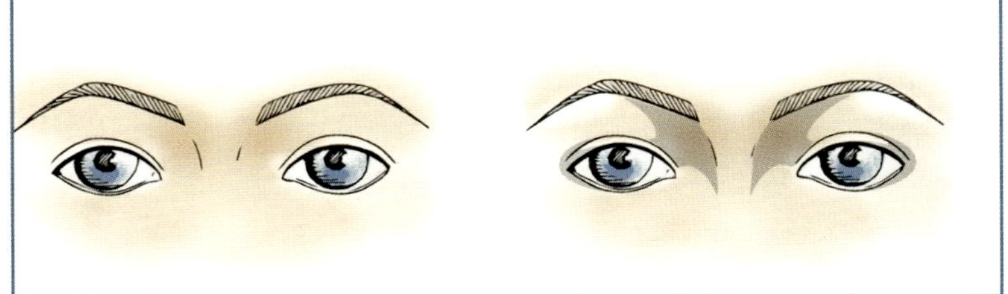

Wide-spaced eyes. For this type of eyes, it makes no difference what makeup pattern to use, the main thing is to accentuate the inner eye corner with dark shadow or shadow of medium saturation. This will shorten the distance between the eyes visually.

Les yeux très écartés. Avec ce type d'yeux, le maquillage pour les yeux que vous allez choisir n'a pas trop d'importance, l'essentiel est de marquer le coin intérieur de l'œil avec des fards à paupières sombres ou des fards d'intensité moyenne. Ceci va raccourcir visuellement la distance entre les yeux.

Weit auseinander stehende Augen. Bei dieser Augenform spielt das Make-up-Muster keine Rolle. Wichtig ist, den inneren Augenwinkel mit einem dunklen Lidschatten oder Lidschatten mit einer mittleren Farbsättigung zu betonen. Somit wird die Distanz zwischen den Augen optisch reduziert.

Ojos muy separados. Para este tipo de ojos, no importa qué modelo de maquillaje se realice, lo más importante es acentuar el borde interior del ojo con una sombra oscura o con una sombra de saturación media. Esto acortará visualmente la distancia entre los ojos.

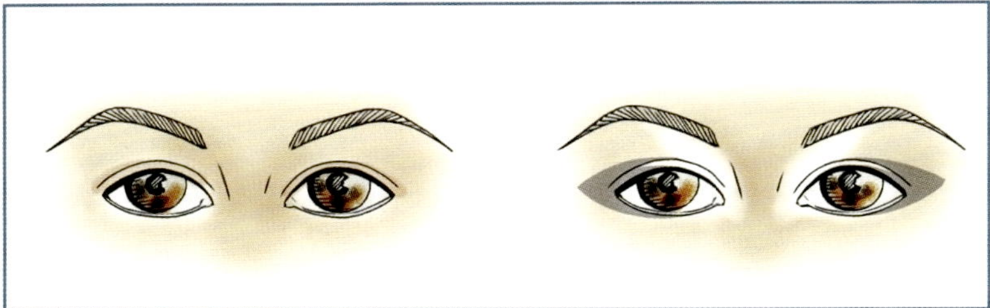

Closely spaced eyes. You can increase the distance between the eyes visually by applying dark or medium shadow to the outer eye corner, and smudging it towards the temple. Highlight the movable lid and inner eye corner with light pearl shadow.

Les yeux très rapprochés. Pour augmenter visuellement la distance entre les yeux, vous pouvez appliquer des fards à paupières sombres ou des fards d'intensité moyenne dans le coin externe de l'œil, et estompez-les en allant vers les parties latérales du front. Appliquez des fards clairs nacrés sur la paupière mobile et dans le coin interne de l'œil.

Eng zusammenstehende Augen. Sie können die Distanz zwischen den Augen optisch vergrößern, indem Sie einen Lidschatten in einem dunklen oder mittleren Farbton auf den äußeren Augenwinkel auftragen und diesen zur Schläfe hin verwischen. Betonen Sie das bewegliche Lid und den inneren Augenwinkel mit einem hellen Lidschatten mit Perlmuttglanz.

Ojos muy juntos. Puedes aumentar visualmente la distancia entre los ojos, al aplicar una sombra, en tono oscuro o medio, en el borde externo del ojo, y esfumarla hacia la sien. Resalta el párpado móvil y el borde interior con una sombra perlada en tono claro.

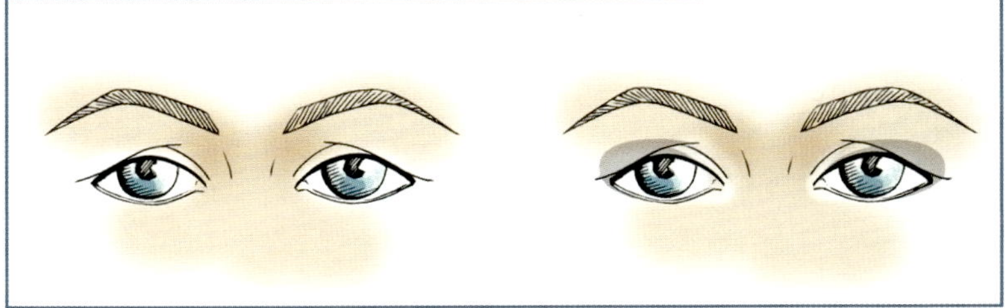

Lowered eyelid. You can correct the lowered lid with the following technique: apply shadow of medium color to the eyelid crease, smudge it towards the eyebrow.

Les paupières abaissées. Il existe une technique pour corriger une paupière abaissée : appliquez des fards d'intensité moyenne dans le pli palpébral et estompez-les ensuite vers les sourcils.

Schlupflider. Schlupflider können folgendermaßen korrigiert werden: Tragen Sie einen Lidschatten in einem mittleren Farbton auf die Lidfalte auf und verwischen Sie diesen zur Augenbraue hin.

Párpado caído. Puedes corregir el párpado caído con la siguiente técnica: aplica una sombra de un tono medio sobre el pliegue del párpado y esfúmala hacia la ceja.

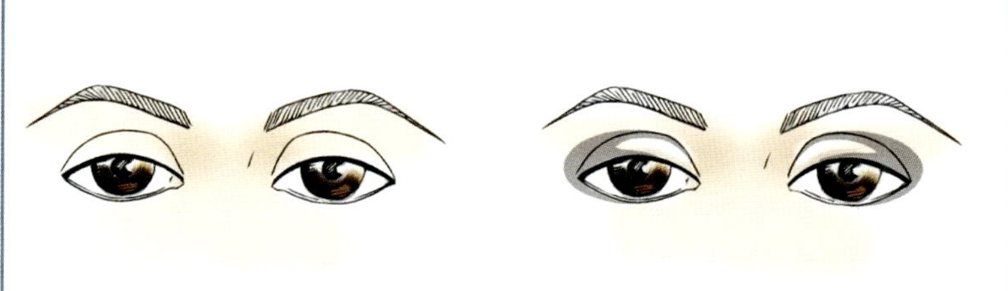

Voluminous movable eyelid. To reduce a too voluminous upper eyelid visually, apply dark shadow along the lash line and the movable eyelid crease connecting it at the outer eye corner. Highlight the inner eye corner and movable lid with light shadow.

Les yeux globuleux. Pour diminuer visuellement une paupière supérieure excessive, étalez les fards à paupières foncés au ras des cils et dans le pli palpébral en les ramenant vers le coin externe de l'œil. Appliquez du fard à paupières clair sur le coin interne de l'œil et sur la paupière mobile.

Voluminöses, bewegliches Augenlid. Um ein voluminöses Augenlid optisch zu verkleinern, trägt man einen dunklen Lidschatten entlang des Wimpernrands und auf das die bewegliche Augenlidfalte auf und verbindet diese im äußeren Augenwinkel. Betonen Sie den inneren Augenwinkel und das bewegliche Augenlid mit einem hellen Lidschatten.

Párpados móviles voluminosos. Para reducir visualmente el volumen del párpado superior, aplicar sombra oscura a lo largo de la línea de las pestañas y del pliegue del párpado móvil, conectándolo en el borde externo del ojo. Realzar el borde interno del ojo y el párpado móvil con una sombra clara.

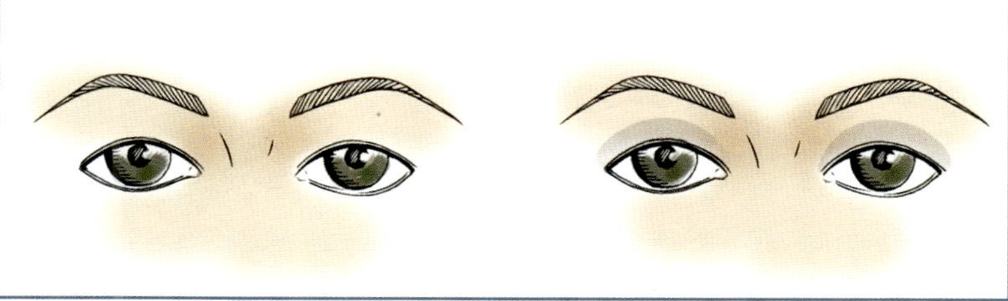

Narrow movable lid. To correct a too narrow movable lid, lay the main emphasis upon the upper eyelid. Accentuate the movable eyelid crease with shadow of dark or medium color, while applying light shadow to the movable lid, inner eye corner and under the eyebrow.

Les yeux bridés. Pour corriger une paupière mobile trop étroite, faites ressortir la paupière supérieure. Appliquez un fard de demi-teinte ou sombre sur le pli palpébral, et des fards clairs sur la paupière mobile, le coin interne de l'œil et sur l'arcade sourcilière.

Kleines bewegliches Augenlid. Um ein kleines bewegliches Augenlid zu korrigieren müssen Sie das obere Augenlid betonen. Heben Sie die Lidfalte des beweglichen Augenlids mit einem Lidschatten in einem dunklen oder mittleren Farbton hervor. Tragen Sie auf das bewegliche Lid, den inneren Augenwinkel und unterhalb der Augenbraue einen hellen Lidschatten auf.

Párpado móvil angosto. Para corregir un párpado móvil demasiado angosto, centrar el mayor énfasis en el párpado superior. Acentuar el pliegue móvil del párpado con una sombra de un color oscuro o medio, en tanto que hay que aplicar, una sombra clara sobre el párpado móvil, en el borde interior del ojo y debajo de las cejas.

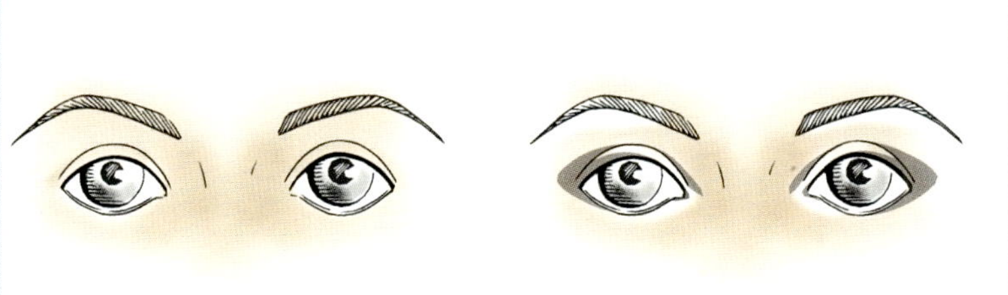

Round eyes. It is very simple to "extend" too round eyes visually: apply shadow of dark or medium intense color to the outer eye corner and smudge it towards the temple. And draw "arrows"!

Les yeux ronds. Pour allonger visuellement des yeux trop ronds, c'est très simple : appliquez des fards à paupières sombres ou des fards d'intensité moyenne dans le coin externe de l'œil et estompez-les en allant vers les tempes. Faites ainsi un effet « œil de biche ».

Runde Augen. Es ist sehr einfach zu runde Augen „zu strecken": Tragen Sie Lidschatten in einem dunklen Farbton oder mittleren Farbtonauf den äußeren Augenwinkel auf und verwischen Sie diesen zur Schläfe hin. Malen Sie „Pfeile"!

Ojos redondos. Es muy simple alargar visualmente un ojo redondo: aplicar una sombra oscura de un color de intensidad media sobre el borde externo del ojo y esfumarla hacia la sien. ¡Trazar "flechas"!

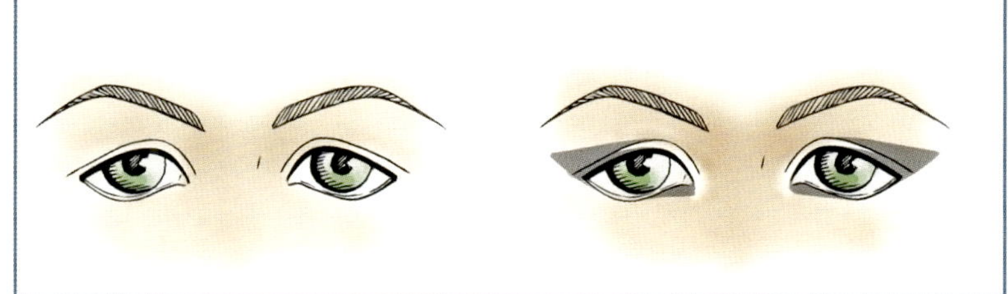

Lowered eye corner. To raise the lowered eye corner, you should "turn the eye around" visually. Do the following: apply dark shadow to the outer eye corner and smudge it upwards. Highlight the lower line of the inner eye with light shadow, movable lid and the area under the eyebrow with light shadow.

Le coin de l'œil abaissé. Afin de rehausser un coin d'œil abaissé, l'œil doit visuellement « pivoter ». Pour ce faire, appliquez des fards à paupières sombres sur le coin supérieur de l'œil et estompez-les vers le haut. Au moyen de fards clairs, marquez la ligne inférieure du coin intérieur de l'œil, la paupière mobile et la zone sous les sourcils.

Hängende Augenwinkel. Um hängende Augenwinkel zu korrigieren, müssen Sie „das Auge optisch umdrehen".Tragen Sie dunklen Lidschatten auf den äußeren Augenwinkel auf und verwischen Sie diesen nach oben hin. Betonen Sie den inneren Augenwinkel, das bewegliche Augenlid und den Bereich unterhalb der Augenbraue mit einem hellen Lidschatten.

Borde caído del ojo. Para levantar el borde caído, habrá que "dar vuelta" visualmente el ojo. Para eso, aplicar sombra oscura en el borde externo del ojo y esfumarla hacia arriba. Resaltar con sombra clara la línea inferior, el párpado móvil y el área bajo las cejas.

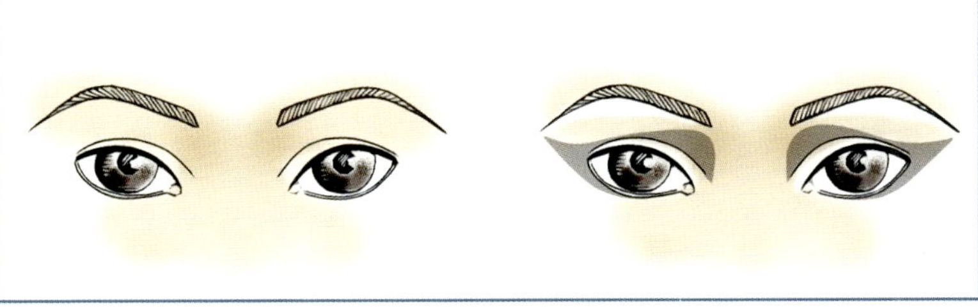

Almond-shaped eyes. To correct this eye shape, accentuate the inner eye corner with dark shadow, smudge it towards the beginning of the eyebrow. Accentuate the outer eye corner along the lower lash line with shadow, smidge the shadow towards the temple.

Les yeux en amande. Pour corriger cette forme d'yeux, faites ressortir le coin interne de l'œil avec des fards sombres et estompez-les en allant vers la base des sourcils. Faites apparaître le coin externe de l'œil le long des cils inférieurs et étalez-les ensuite vers les tempes.

Mandelförmige Augen. Um diese Augenform zu korrigieren, muss der innere Augenwinkel mit einem dunklen Lidschatten betont werden. Verwischen Sie diesen zur Augenbraue hin. Betonen Sie den äußeren Augenwinkel, entlang des unteren Wimpernrands mit Lidschatten und verwischen Sie diesen zur Schläfe hin.

Ojos almendrados. Para corregir esta forma de ojo, acentúa el borde interno con una sombra oscura, esfúmala hacia el comienzo de las cejas. Destaca el borde externo del ojo a lo largo de la línea de las pestañas inferiores con una sombra, difuminarla hacia la sien.

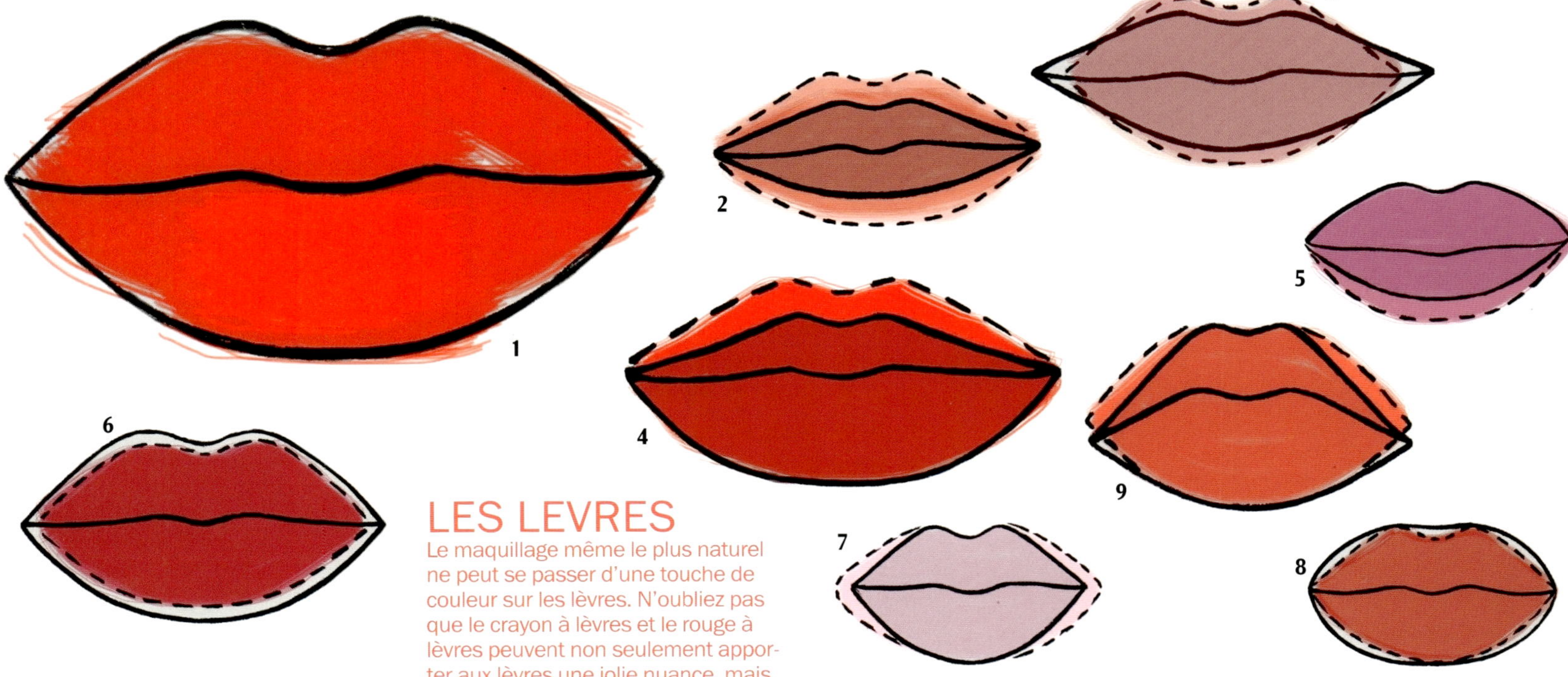

LIPS

Even the most natural make-up cannot do without a color accent on the lips. However, a liner and a lipstick are capable of not only giving a nice shade to the lips, but also correct their shape visually.

1. From the makeup artist's point of view, ideal lips have an equal width, and are absolutely symmetrical from both right and left sides. They are few and far between.
2. Thin lips. Draw a line with a lip liner a little above the natural line of the upper and lower lips. Notice: do not accentuate the outer lip corners.
3. Long lips. While contouring the lips, at the center draw a line a little above the upper lip and a little below the lower one. Notice: the line should not reach the lip corners.
4. Narrow upper line. Increase the upper lip with a lip liner so that it will be visually equal to the width of the lower one. If the lower lips is heavy, "raise" the contour a little.
5. Narrow lower lip. Increase the lower lip with a lip liner so that it will be visually equal to the width of the upper one. If the upper lip is very heavy, "lower" the contour 1-2 mm downwards.
6. Small, too "round" lips. Contouring the lips, color the upper and lower lips minimally, while coloring the outer eye corner maximally, up to the very extreme points of the lips.
7. Large lips. Contour lips, stepping back slightly to reduce the lip size. Only lips of little pigmentation and relief can be corrected considerably.
8. Blurry lip shape. Imagine the ideal lip shape and draw a clearer line following it: draw clear corners and an upper lip "arch", then a lower lip line; finally, direct both lines towards the outer corners.
9. Lowered lip corners. Start drawing from the lower lip contour trying to direct the line upwards. Place small marks on the upper lips little above the lowered corners and direct the upper lip line towards them.

LES LEVRES

Le maquillage même le plus naturel ne peut se passer d'une touche de couleur sur les lèvres. N'oubliez pas que le crayon à lèvres et le rouge à lèvres peuvent non seulement apporter aux lèvres une jolie nuance, mais aussi corriger visuellement leur forme.

1. Du point de vue d'un visagiste, les lèvres idéales sont toutes deux de la même épaisseur et sont tout à fait symétriques. Ce type idéal de lèvres se rencontre assez rarement.
2. Les lèvres fines. Dessinez le contour des lèvres au-dessus de la ligne naturelle de la lèvre supérieure et un peu en dessous de la lèvre inférieure avec un crayon à lèvres. Attention à ne pas l'appliquer dans les commissures des lèvres.
3. Les lèvres longues. En dessinant le contour, remontez la ligne au milieu des lèvres, au-dessus du creux de la lèvre supérieure et également abaissez légèrement la ligne de la lèvre inférieure. Faites attention à ne pas aller jusqu'aux commissures des lèvres.
4. La lèvre supérieure fine. Augmentez l'épaisseur de la lèvre supérieure avec un crayon à lèvres pour qu'elle corresponde visuellement à l'épaisseur de la lèvre inférieure. Si la lèvre inférieure est charnue, remontez son contour légèrement vers le haut.
5. La lèvre inférieure fine. Augmentez l'épaisseur de la lèvre inférieure avec un crayon à lèvres pour qu'elle corresponde visuellement à l'épaisseur de la lèvre supérieure. Si la lèvre supérieure est très charnue, abaissez son contour légèrement vers le bas de 1 à 2 mm.
6. Les lèvres petites et trop rondes. Dessinez légèrement le contour des lèvres supérieure et inférieure, mettez plutôt l'accent sur les commissures des lèvres en les faisant ressortir jusqu'aux extrémités.
7. Les lèvres charnues. Dessinez le contour des lèvres, en faisant un retrait du contour naturel des lèvres. Il n'y a que des lèvres à la pigmentation et au relief peu prononcés qui peuvent bénéficier d'une correction significative.
8. Les lèvres aux contours flous. Pensez à la forme idéale des lèvres et dessinez une ligne plus nette en vous tenant à cette forme. Commencez par les commissures des lèvres, suivez le contour de l'arc de Cupidon sur la lèvre supérieure, puis dessinez la ligne de la lèvre inférieure, et reliez chaque côté de l'arc de Cupidon jusqu'au bord de chaque commissure des lèvres.
9. Les lèvres aux coins abaissés. Commencez par dessiner le contour de la lèvre inférieure, en le remontant vers le haut. Marquez des points sur la lèvre supérieure légèrement au-dessus des coins des lèvres abaissés et reliez-les avec chaque côté de la lèvre supérieure.

LIPPEN

Auch das natürlichste Make-up braucht einen Farbakzent auf den Lippen. Lipliner und Lippenstift verleihen Lippen nicht nur eine tolle Form sondern korrigierenauch die Lippenform optisch.

1. Aus Sicht des Visagisten haben perfekte Lippen das gleiche Volumen und sind auf beiden Seiten absolut symmetrisch. Das ist allerdings nur selten der Fall.
2. Dünne Lippen. Ziehen Sie die Linie mit dem Lipliner etwas oberhalb der natürlichen Ober- und Unterlippenlinie. Hinweis: Betonen Sie die äußeren Mundwinkel nicht.
3. Lange Lippen. Wenn Sie die Lippen nachziehen, ziehen Sie die Konturen in der Mitte der Oberlippe etwas höher und etwas tiefer unterhalb der Unterlippe nach. Hinweis: Die Konturlinie sollte nicht bis zu den Mundwinkeln reichen.
4. Schmale Oberlippe. Verleihen Sie der Oberlippe mit einem Lipliner mehr Volumen, um optisch die Breite der Unterlippe zu erreichen. Bei einer ausgeprägten Unterlippe müssen die Konturen etwas „angehoben" werden.
5. Schmale Unterlippe. Verleihen Sie der Unterlippe mit einem Lipliner mehr Volumen, um optisch die Breite der Oberlippe zu erreichen. Bei einer ausgeprägten Oberlippe müssen die Konturen etwa 1-2 mm „gesenkt" werden.
6. Schmale, zu „runde" Lippen. Ziehen Sie die Konturen der Lippen nach und tragen Sie nur wenig Farbe auf die Ober- und Unterlippe auf. Tragen Sie großzügigLidschatten auf das äußere Augenwinkel auf und ziehen Sie diese auf die Höhe der äußeren Wundwinkel.
7. Große Lippen. Ziehen Sie die Lippenkonturen etwas kleiner nach, um die Lippengröße zu verringern. Nur Lippen mit wenig Pigmentierung können in ihrer Größe wesentlich korrigiert werden.
8. Undeutliche Lippenkonturen. Stellen Sie sich die perfekte Lippenform vor und ziehen Sie eine deutliche Linie in folgender Reihenfolge: Mundwinkel, Armorbogen, Unterlippe und zuletzt beide Oberlippenlinien zum Mundwinkel hin.
9. Hängende Mundwinkel. Beginnen Sie mit der Unterlippenkontur und versuchen Sie die Linie etwas nach oben zu ziehen. Markieren Sie etwas über den hängenden Mundwinkeln kleine Punkte auf der Oberlippe und ziehen Sie die obere Lippenlinie in diese Richtung.

LABIOS

Por natural que sea el maquillaje, no puede no destacar los labios. Porque el lápiz delineador y el labial son capaces no solo de dar un tono agradable, sino también corregir las imperfecciones.

1. Desde el punto de vista del maquillaje artístico, los labios ideales tienen igual ancho y son absolutamente simétricos a ambos lados, el derecho y el izquierdo. ¡Acaso hay alguno!
2. Labios angostos. Trazar una línea con un lápiz delineador arriba de la línea natural del labio superior y del inferior. Nota: no acentuar el borde externo.
3. Labios alargados. Mientras se contornea el labio, en el centro, trazar una línea arriba del labio superior y un poco debajo del labio inferior. Nota: la línea no debe llegar hasta el borde de los labios.
4. Línea superior angosta: Aumentar el labio superior con un delineador para que luzcan ambos labios iguales. Si el labio inferior es grueso, contornear un poco adentro del labio.
5. Labio inferior angosto. Aumentar el labio inferior con un delineador para que el ancho de ambos labios luzca similar. Si el labio superior es muy pronunciado, contornearlo a 1-2 mm por dentro.
6. Labios pequeños y redondos. Contornear los labios, pintando apenas el labio superior y el inferior, mientras se pinta mucho el borde externo del ojo hasta las puntas del labio.
7. Labios grandes. Contornear los labios por dentro de la línea natural para reducir el tamaño. Los labios con poca pigmentación pueden corregirse considerablemente.
8. Labios de forma difusa. Imaginar la forma de ladios ideal y trazar una línea clara siguiéndola: trazar bordes definidos y el arco del labio superior, luego la línea del labio inferior; finalmente trazar las líneas hacia los bordes.
9. Labios con bordes caídos. Comenzar a trazar el contorno desde el borde inferior, dirigiendo las líneas hacia arriba. Colocar pequeñas marcas sobre el labio superior, apenas arriba del borde inferior y dirigir la línea del labio superior hacia ellas.

EYEBROWS

"A beautiful woman must have beautiful eyebrow" – joke makeup artists. Indeed, your eyebrows are a question of not only makeup, but also your personality, if you like. That is why it is so important to give them a proper shape – one that will perfectly match the facial features.

1. An eyebrow of rounded shape is the most regular, feminine variant. This shape will be suitable for owners of an oval shape with soft features.
2. A graphic eyebrow is characterized by harsher lines and a more definite bend. Eyebrows of that shape are good to correct wide faces: round, square, pear-shaped ones.
3. A straight eyebrow line with a smooth, non-definite (unexpressed) bend will match narrow, drawn, thin faces. This eyebrow shape will widen them visually.

Eyebrow color should match the color type of your appearance and your hair color. Ideally, the color of the eyebrow should be equal to, or a tone darker than the hair color. It is vital that the eyebrow color and hair shade are of the same "temperature" palette: for example, eyebrows of a warm shade will match hair of a cold tone badly, and vice versa.

LES SOURCILS

« A belle femme, beaux sourcils », plaisantent les visagistes. C'est pourtant vrai, les sourcils ne sont pas tellement liés avec le maquillage, mais, si vous voulez, plutôt avec votre personnalité. C'est pourquoi il est si important de leur donner une forme correcte, qui correspond parfaitement aux traits du visage

1. Les sourcils aux contours arrondis sont les plus adaptés et les plus féminins. Cette forme convient aux femmes au visage ovale et aux traits doux.
2. Les sourcils graphiques se distinguent par leur ligne oblique, plus dessinée et franche. Les sourcils de cette forme conviennent très bien aux visages ronds, carrés et hexagonaux.
3. La ligne droite du sourcil à la courbe douce, peu prononcée, convient aux visages étroits, allongés et minces. Cette forme des sourcils les élargit visuellement.

La couleur des sourcils doit être adaptée à la carnation et à la teinte des cheveux. Idéalement, la couleur des sourcils doit être celle des cheveux ou d'une teinte plus foncée. Il est très important que la couleur des sourcils et la teinte des cheveux soient du même coloris : les sourcils d'une teinte chaude n'iront pas bien avec les cheveux d'une teinte froide et vice versa.

AUGENBRAUEN

„ Eine schöne Frau braucht schöne Augenbrauen" – scherzen Visagisten. Ihre Augenbrauen sind nicht nur Teil Ihres Make-ups sondern auch Ihrer Persönlichkeit. Von daher ist es besonders wichtig, ihnen die richtige Form zu verleihen, die perfekt zu Ihrem Gesicht passt.

1. Augenbrauen mit rundem Bogen sind die weitverbreitete, weibliche Variante. Diese Augenbrauenform eignet sich für ovale Gesichtsformen mit weichen Gesichtszügen.
2. Eine extravagante Augenbraue zeichnet sich durch strengere Linien und einen ausgeprägten Bogen aus. Diese Augenbrauenform eignet sich gut dazu, um breite (d. h. runde, eckige, birnenförmige) Gesichter zu verschmälern.
3. Eine gerade Augenbrauenlinie mit einem weichen, unausgeprägten (leichten) Bogen eignet sich für schmale, feine, dünne Gesichtsformen. Diese Augenbrauenform lässt diese Gesichtsformen optisch breiter erscheinen.

Die Augenbrauenfarbe sollte zu Ihrer Gesichts- und Haarfarbe passen. Idealerweise sollte die Augenbrauenfarbe den gleichen Farbton oder einen Farbton dunkler als Ihre Haarfarbe sein. Es ist wichtig, dass die Augenbrauenfarbe und Haarfarbe aus der gleichen Farbpalette stammen. Dementsprechend ist ein warmer Farbton nicht für kalte Farbtöne, und umgekehrt, geeignet.

CEJAS

" Una mujer bella debe tener bellas cejas"– dicen los maquilladores atísticos. Claro que las cejas no son solo una cuestión de maquillaje, sino también de personalidad, si se quiere. Es por eso que es tan importante darles la forma adecuada – la forma que cuadre perfectamente con las características faciales.

1. Una ceja de forma redondeada es la variante regular más femenina. Esta forma es adecuada para las personas que poseen una cara ovalada con suaves rasgos.
2. Las cejas gráficas se caracterizan por líneas duras y un arco definido. Este tipo de cejas son buenas para corregir caras amplias: redondas, cuadradas, y con forma de pera.
3. La ceja en línea recta con una suave, no definida (inexpresiva) curva combina con caras angostas, enjutas y finas. Esta forma de cejas harán que la cara parezca más amplia.

El color de las cejas debe combinar el color de la apariencia general y del cabello. Idealmente, el color de las cejas debe ser igual al del pelo, o un tono más oscuro. Es vital que el color de la ceja y el tono del pelo sean de la misma "temperatura" por ejemplo, si las cejas son de un tono cálido apenas combinará con un tono de pelo frío y viceversa.

CLASSIC MAKE-UP OFFERS TIME PROVED SOLUTIONS AND IDEAL COLOR COMBINATIONS. IF YOU MASTER CLASSIC MAKE-UP TECHNIQUES, YOU WILL ALWAYS BE "FULLY ARMED" – THEY ARE SUITABLE FOR ANY OCCASION AND FOR ANY TYPE OF APPEARANCE.

LE MAQUILLAGE CLASSIQUE, CE SONT DES IDÉES QUI ONT RÉSISTÉ À L'ÉPREUVE DU TEMPS ET DES ACCORDS DE COULEURS IDÉAUX. APRÈS AVOIR APPRIS LA TECHNIQUE DE MAQUILLAGE CLASSIQUE, VOUS SEREZ TOUJOURS « ARMÉE » CAR IL CONVIENT À TOUTE OCCASION ET À TOUT TYPE DE VISAGE.

KLASSISCHES MAKE-UP BESTEHT AUS BEWÄHRTEN LÖSUNGEN UND IDEALEN FARBKOMBINATIONEN. WENN SIE DIE KLASSISCHEN MAKE-UP-TECHNIKEN BEHERRSCHEN, SIND SIE IMMER "VOLL AUSGERÜSTET" – FÜR JEDE GELEGENHEIT UND JEDES OUTFIT.

EL MAQUILLAJE CLÁSICO ES UNA SOLUCIÓN A PRUEBA DEL TIEMPO Y UNA COMBINACIÓN IDEAL DE COLORES. SI DOMINAS LAS TÉCNICAS DEL MAQUILLAJE CLÁSICO, ESTARÁS "COMPLETAMENTE EQUIPADA" YA QUE SON ADECUADAS EN CUALQUIER OCASIÓN Y EN TODO TIPO DE APARIENCIA.

PURE ENERGY

ENGLISH

To even the skin tone, apply light reflecting foundation. **2.** Accentuate the natural line of the eyebrows with translucent gel. **3.** Apply pale beige shadow to the upper and lower eyelids. **4.** Apply brown mascara with golden shade to the eyelashes. **5.** Contour the lips with a ruby pencil following their natural shape. **6.** Apply a carroty red lip color to the lips. **7.** To finish the makeup, apply bronzing rouge.

FRANÇAIS

1. Pour unifier le teint du visage, appliquez un fond de teint matifiant à fines particules réflectrices de lumière. **2.** Gainez les sourcils avec un gel capillaire incolore en gardant leur ligne naturelle. **3.** Appliquez les fards à paupières beige pâle sur la totalité des paupières supérieures et inférieures. **4.** Utilisez un mascara brun doré. **5.** Dessinez bien le contour des lèvres à l'aide d'un crayon rouge vif en suivant leur contour naturel. **6.** Remplissez les lèvres avec un rouge à lèvres de couleur rouge orangé. **7.** Finalisez le maquillage avec un blush effet bronzé.

DEUTSCH

1. Tragen Sie einelichtreflektierende Foundation für einen ebenmäßigen Teint auf. **2.** Betonen Sie die natürliche Form der Augenbrauen mit einem transparenten Gel. **3.** Tragen Sie einen blassen beigefarbenen Lidschatten auf die Ober- und Unterlider auf. **4.** Tragen Sie eine braune Mascara mit Goldton auf die Wimpern auf. **5.** Ziehen Sie die natürliche Kontur der Lippen mit einem rubinroten Lipliner nach. **6.** Verwenden Sie einen karrottenroten Lippenstift. **7.** Vervollständigen Sie das Make-up mit einem Bronzing Rouge.

ESPAÑOL

1. Para emparejar el tono de la piel, aplicar una base luminosa. **2.** Acentuar la línea natural de las cejas con un gel translúcido. **3.** Aplicar una sombra beige a los párpados superiores e inferiores. **4.** Aplicar máscara marrón con tonos dorados en las pestañas **5.** Contornear los labios con un lápiz de color rubí, siguiendo su forma natural. **6.** Aplicar un labial de color rojo zanahoria a los labios. **7.** Para finalizar el maquillaje, aplicar un rouge color bronce.

1

2

3

4

5

6

7

Model: Margarita Kochkina @ Fashion

TEMPTATION

ENGLISH

1. To even the complexion, apply matte foundation close to the skin tone. Correct the facial contours and nose shape with powder of two shades. **2.** Accentuate the upper movable lid and the area under the eyebrow with white matte shadow. **3.** Accentuate the natural eyebrow line with a taupe pencil, style the eyebrows with transparent gel in the proper direction. **4.** Apply brown shadow to the outer eye corner highlighting the upper eyelid crease and the outer corner of the lower eyelid to get a V-shape. **5.** Accentuating the outer eye corner, draw a line with a black pencil from the middle of the lower eyelid and contour the upper lid, extend the pencil line with a clear arrow in the outer eye corner. Apply black mascara to the eyelashes. **6.** Apply coral gloss to the lips. **7.** To refresh the face, use pale pink rouge.

FRANÇAIS

1. Pour unifier le teint du visage, appliquez un fond de teint matifiant, à la couleur identique à la carnation de la peau. Corrigez l'ovale du visage et le nez en les balayant avec des poudres de deux teints. **2.** Eclaircissez la paupière mobile en appliquant des fards à paupières blancs mats. Appliquez-les également sur l'arcade sourcilière. **3.** Marquez le contour des sourcils avec un crayon gris-brun en suivant leur ligne naturelle, gainez-les au gel capillaire incolore pour les discipliner dans le sens souhaité. **4.** Appliquez des ombres à paupières brunes dans le coin externe de l'œil en faisant ressortir le pli palpébral de la paupière supérieure et le coin externe de la paupière inférieure pour former la lettre « V ». **5.** Dessinez un trait partant du milieu de la paupière inférieure avec un crayon noir et sur la totalité de la paupière supérieure en accentuant le coin externe de l'œil. Continuez le trait en créant un petit crochet net, pour faire un « œil de biche ». Mettez un mascara noir sur les cils. **6.** Appliquez un brillant couleur corail sur les lèvres. **7.** Pour rehausser l'éclat du visage posez des fards à joues rose pâle.

DEUTSCH

1. Tragen Sie eine matte Foundation für einen ebenmäßigen Teint auf. Korrigieren Sie die Gesichtskonturen und Nasenform mit Pudern in zwei Farbtönen. **2.** Betonen Sie das bewegliche Oberlid und den Bereich unterhalb der Augenbraue mit einem matten weißen Lidschatten. **3.** Betonen Sie die natürliche Form der Augenbrauen mit einem graubraunen Augenbrauenstift und stylen Sie die Augenbrauen mit einem transparenten Gel. **4.** Tragen Sie braunen Lidschatten auf den äußeren Augenwinkel auf und betonen Sie dabei die obere Augenlidfalte und den äußeren Winkel des Unterlids, um eine V-Form zu erhalten. **5.** Ziehen Sie mit einem schwarzen Stift eine Linie von der Mitte des unteren Augenlids aus und ziehen Sie das Oberlid nach, um den äußeren Augenwinkel zu betonen. Erweitern Sie die gezogene Linie mit einem deutlichen Pfeil im äußeren Augenwinkel. Tragen Sie Mascara auf. **6.** Tragen Sie ein korallfarbenes Lipgloss auf. **7.** Verwenden Sie ein blassrosa Rouge um einen frischen Look zu erhalten.

ESPAÑOL

1. Para emparejar el cutis, aplicar una base mate de un tono semejante al de la piel. Corregir el contorno facial y la forma de la nariz con polvo de dos tonos. **2.** Acentuar el párpado superior móvil y el área debajo de las cejas con una sombra mate de color blanco. **3.** Acentuar la línea natural de la ceja con un lápiz marrón topo, modelar las cejas con un gel transparente en la dirección adecuada. **4.** Aplicar una sombra marrón al borde externo de ojo resaltando el pliegue del párpado superior y el borde externo del párpado inferior para obtener un forma de V **5.** Acentuar el borde externo del ojo, trazar una línea con un lápiz negro desde el centro del párpado inferior y el contorno del párpado superior, extender la línea del lápiz con una nítida flecha en el borde externo del ojo. Aplicar Máscara negra a las pestañas. **6.** Aplicar brillo de color coral a los labios. **7.** Para realzar la cara usar un rouge rosa pálido.

1

2

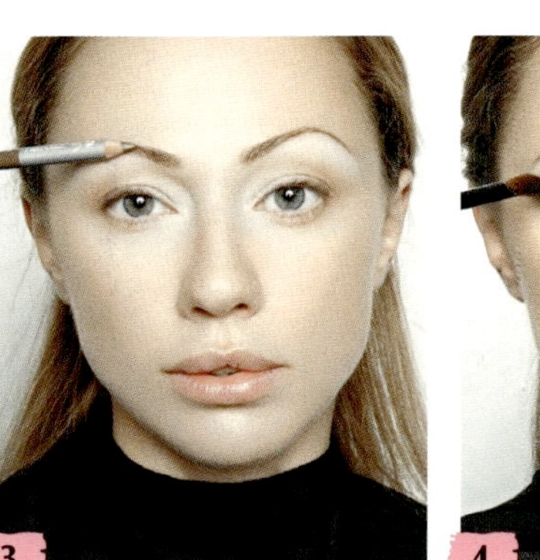
3

4

5

6

7

Model: Lika Pimenova

QUEEN OF THE BALL

ENGLISH

1. Even out the skin texture with light reflecting foundation. To make the skin slightly shine, apply light concealer close to the natural skin tone. **2.** To even the skin use golden bronzing powder. **3.** Accentuate the natural eyebrow shape with a beige pencil. **4.** Apply subtle bronze pearlescent shadow to the upper eyelid and to the inner eye corner. **5.** Apply bright violet shadow to the upper movable lid. **6.** Accentuate the upper and lower lids with a black greasy eyeliner just at the eyelashes, contour the corner of the upper movable lid in the same way. This will be the foundation for the makeup. **7.** Apply dark brown golden shadow to the lower and upper immovable eyelids. Shade it, highlighting the outer eye corner and accentuating the round shape of the upper lid. **8.** To refresh the face, use slightly glossy rouge of natural color. **9.** Apply volume mascara to the eyelashes. To make the sight more impressive, contour the eye from inside with a black pencil. **10.** As a finishing touch, apply transparent gloss of cold shade to the lips.

FRANÇAIS

1. Egaliser le teint du visage en appliquant une base de maquillage aux particules réflectrices de lumière. Etalez un fond de teint de couleur proche de celle de la carnation, ce qui rendra le teint légèrement lumineux. **2.** Rendez la peau plus lisse à l'aide d'une poudre or brillant à effet bronzage naturel. **3.** Dessinez les sourcils avec un crayon beige en soulignant leur forme naturelle. **4.** Appliquez des ombres à paupières bronze pâle nacré sur la paupière supérieure et le coin interne de l'œil. **5.** Teintez la paupière mobile avec des ombres à paupières prune vif. **6.** Tracez une ligne au ras des cils supérieurs et inférieurs à l'aide d'un crayon gras noir. Dessinez de la même façon l'angle de la paupière mobile. Cela servira de base pour la suite du maquillage. **7.** Appliquez des ombres à paupières brun foncé avec des reflets dorés sur la paupière inférieure et sur l'arcade sourcilière. Estompez-les en mettant l'accent sur le coin externe de l'œil pour accentuer l'arrondi de la paupière supérieure. **8.** Rehaussez l'éclat du visage en étalant des fards à joues identiques à la couleur naturelle au brillant/nacré léger. **9.** Complétez le maquillage des yeux avec un mascara effet volume. Pour intensifier le regard dessinez un trait au crayon noir près des cils à l'intérieur de l'œil. **10.** Finalisez le maquillage en mettant un gloss de teint froid sur les lèvres.

DEUTSCH

1. Tragen Sie eine lichtreflektierende Foundation für einen ebenmäßigen Teint auf. Verwenden Sie einen hellen Concealer, der eine Nuance heller ist als Ihr Hautton, um einen frischen Teint zu erhalten. **2.** Verwenden Sie einen goldfarbenenBronzing-Puder. **3.** Betonen Sie die natürliche Augenbrauenform mit einem beigefarbenen Stift. **4.** Tragen Sie einen dezenten bronzefarbenen Lidschatten mit Perlmuttglanz auf das Oberlid und den inneren Augenwinkel auf. **5.** Tragen Sie hellvioletten Lidschatten auf das bewegliche Oberlid auf. **6.** Betonen Sie das Ober- und Unterlid mit einem schwarzen,leicht verschmierenden Eyeliner am Wimpernansatz. Ziehen Sie die Augenkontur des Oberlids nach. Das ist Ihre Make-up-Basis. **7.** Tragen Sie einen dunkelbraunen mit Goldtönen versetzten Lidschatten auf die unbeweglichen Ober- und Unterlider auf. Betonen Sie somit den äußeren Augenwinkel und die runde Augenform des Oberlids. **8.** Verwenden Sie ein natürliches, leicht glänzendes Rouge für einen frischen Teint. **9.** Tragen Sie Volume-Mascara auf. Um den Look zu verstärken, können Sie die inneren Wimpernränder mit einem schwarzen Stift nachziehen. **10.** Vervollständigen Sie den Look mit einem transparenten Lipgloss in einer kühlen Farbe.

ESPAÑOL

1.Emparejar la textura de la piel con una base luminosa. Para darle a la piel un aspecto algo brilloso, aplicar un corrector de un tono semejante al de la piel. **2.** Para emparejar la piel, utilizar polvo dorado bronceado. **3.** Acentuar la forma natural de la ceja con un lápiz beige. **4.** Aplicar una sombra color bronce con un sutil tono perlado al párpado superior y al borde interno del ojo. **5.** aplicar una sombra violeta al párpado superior móvil. **6.** Acentuar los párpados superiores e inferiores con un delineador graso negro, justo en la naciente de las pestañas, contornear el borde del párpado superior móvil de la misma manera. Esta será la base del maquillaje. **7.** Aplicar una sombra dorada marrón oscura a los párpados superiores e inferiores fijos. Pintarlos resaltando el borde externo del ojo y la forma redondeada del párpado superior. **8.** Para realzar la cara, utilizar un rouge apenas brilloso de un color natural. **9.** Aplicar una máscara efecto volumen en las pestañas. Para lograr una mirada más interesante, contornear el ojo desde adentro con un lápiz negro. **10.** Como toque final, aplicar brillo transparente de un tono frío a los labios.

1

2

3

4

5

6

7

8

9

10

Model: Yulia Elskaya

PERFECT BORDEAUX

ENGLISH

1. Even out skin tone using a light-reflecting foundation with a luminescent effect that matches skin tone. **2.** Apply beige pearlescent eye-shadow to the eyelids to increase the eye shape visually. **3.** Accentuate the eyebrow line with hazel colored matte eye shadow. **4.** Use lengthening mascara to color eyelashes for contrast. **5.** Apply pearlescent pink-nude tone blusher to the cheekbones to complete the neutral, pearly palette. **6.** Contour the lips with a maroon pencil to slightly round out their shape. **7.** Apply a deep maroon glossy lip color to the lips.

RANÇAIS

1. Pour égaliser la texture de la peau et apporter de la luminosité au visage, appliquez un fond de teint à fines particules réflectrices de lumière à la couleur proche du teint de la peau. **2.** Etalez des ombres à paupières beige nacré, ce qui augmentera visuellement les yeux. **3.** Tracez les sourcils avec un applicateur à ombres à paupières mat de couleur brun clair. **4.** Appliquez un mascara noir effet volume sur les cils. **5.** Etalez des fards à joues rose pâle sur les pommettes. **6.** Marquez le contour des lèvres avec un crayon bordeaux foncé en arrondissant légèrement leur forme. **7.** Remplissez les lèvres avec un gloss de couleur bordeaux foncé.

DEUTSCH

1.Verwenden Sie eine lichtreflektierende Foundation, die zu Ihrem Hautton passt, um einen ebenmäßigen Teint mit einem lumineszierenden Effekt zu erhalten. **2.** Tragen Sie einen beigefarbenenLidschatten mit Perlmuttschimmer auf, um die Augenform optisch zu vergrößern. **3.** Betonen Sie die Augenbrauenlinie mit einem matten, haselnussbraunen Lidschatten. **4.** Betonen Sie die Wimpern mit einer wimpernverlängernden Mascara. **5.** Tragen Sie Rouge in einem Nude-Ton mit Perlmuttschimmer auf die Wangenknochen auf, um den neutralen Perlmutt-Look zu vervollständigen. **6.** Umranden Sie die Lippen mit einem bordeauxroten Konturenstift, um diese voller erscheinen zu lassen. **7.** Tragen Sie zum Abschluss ein bordeauxrotes Lipgloss auf.

ESPAÑOL

1. Emparejar el tono de la piel usando una base luminosa con un efecto resplandeciente que combine con el tono de la piel. **2.** Aplicar una sombra beige perlada a los párpados para aumentar visualmente la forma. **3.** Acentuar la línea de la ceja con una sombra mate de color avellana. **4.** Utilizar una máscara para pintar las pestañas y generar contraste. **5.** Aplicar un rubor perlado de tono rosa piel en los pómulos para completar la paleta perlada neutra. **6.** Contornear los labios con lápiz granate para apenas rellenar su forma. **7.** Aplicar brillo labial de color granate profundo a los labios.

Model: Ekaterina Ukhanova

HOLLYWOOD STAR

ENGLISH

1. Apply light reflecting foundation to the face. **2.** Apply light corrective concealer to problem areas of skin and under the eyes. **3.** To even the complexion, use a matte foundation. **4.** Apply natural tone powder. Correct the face shape with darker powder. **5.** Emphasize the eyebrow lines with grey and brown pencil. **6.** Emphasize the upper eyelid with brown eye shadow making its shape rounder and stretching the outer corner of the eye. Smudge the shadow leaving clear the line that goes from the outer corner; it should visually continue the lower eyelid line. **7.** Draw an arrow with black eye shadow on the upper lid along the whole lash line. Smudge the black shadow to get a V-shape, emphasizing the outer eye corner and lifting it up visually, leaving the lower shade line clear. **8.** Accentuate the upper movable lid with white pearl powdery eye shadow. **9.** Apply volumizing mascara to the eyelashes. **10.** Apply pale-pink blusher to the cheekbones. To finish the look, use a pale-pink lipstick.

FRANÇAIS

1. Appliquez sur le visage une base de maquillage à fines particules réflectrices de lumière. **2.** Appliquez un correcteur clair sur les zones à imperfections de la peau et sous les yeux. **3.** Pour unifier le teint du visage, utilisez un fond de teint matifiant. **4.** Appliquez une poudre de ton naturel. Avec une poudre plus foncée, adoucissez les traits du visage. **5.** Soulignez le contour des sourcils à l'aide d'un crayon gris-brun. **6.** Avec des ombres à paupières brunes faites ressortir la paupière supérieure en l'arrondissant et en étirant le coin externe de l'œil. Estompez les ombres en laissant une ligne nette qui part du coin extérieur de l'œil, elle doit prolonger visuellement la ligne de la paupière inférieure. **7.** A l'aide d'ombres à paupières noires dessinez un trait sur la paupière supérieure en suivant toute la ligne de croissance des cils. Estompez les ombres noires en formant la lettre « V », en soulignant le coin externe de l'œil et en le relevant visuellement, tout en laissant le trait bien net. **8.** Accentuez la paupière supérieure avec un halo d'ombres blanc nacré. **9.** Pour les cils utilisez un mascara noir effet volume. **10.** Appliquez un fard à joues rose pâle sur les pommettes. Finalisez le maquillage avec un rouge à lèvres rose pâle.

DEUTSCH

1. Tragen Sie eine lichtreflektierende Foundation auf. **2.** Kaschieren Sie Problemzonen im Gesicht und unter den Augen mit einem lichtreflektierenden Concealer. **3.** Verwenden Sie eine mattierende Foundation, um einen ebenmäßigen Teint zu erhalten. **4.** Tragen Sie einen Puder in einem natürlichen Farbton auf. Korrigieren Sie Ungleichmäßigkeiten der Gesichtsform mit dunklerem Puder. **5.** Betonen sie die Augenbrauenlinien mit einem grauen und braunen Augenbrauenstift. **6.** Betonen Sie das obere Augenlied mit braunem Lidschatten, um dessen Form runder erscheinen zu lassen und den äußeren Augenwinkel optisch zu strecken. Verwischen Sie den Lidschatten, belassen Sie dabei jedoch die deutliche Linie zum äußeren Augenwinkel. Die Linie des unteren Augenlids sollte somit verlängert erscheinen. **7.** Zeichnen Sie mit schwarzem Lidschatten einen Pfeil auf das obere Augenlid, entlang des gesamten Wimpernrands. Verwischen Sie den schwarzen Lidschatten, um eine V-Form zu erhalten, die den äußeren Augenwinkel betont und diesen optisch anhebt. Die untere Linie bleibt zu sehen. **8.** Betonen Sie das obere bewegliche Augenlid mit einem puderigen, perlweißen Lidschatten. **9.** Tragen Sie Mascara für voluminöse Wimpern auf. **10.** Tragen Sie einen blass-pinken Rougeton auf Ihre Wangenknochen auf. Vervollständigen Sie den Look mit einem blass-pinken Lippenstift.

ESPAÑOL

1. Aplicar una base luminosa a la cara. **2.** Aplicar corrector a las áreas problemáticas de la piel y bajo los ojos. **3.** Para emparejar el cutis, usar una base mate. **4.** Aplicar polvo en tono natural. Corregir la forma de la cara con un polvo más oscuro. **5.** Enfatizar las líneas de las cejas con un lápiz gris marrón. **6.** Resaltar el párpado superior con sombra marrón dándole una forma más redondeada, alargándose hacia el borde externo del ojo. Esfumar la sombra dejando libre la línea que va desde el borde externo; debe continuar visualmente la línea del párpado inferior. **7.** Trazar un arco con sombra negra en el párpado superior a lo largo de la línea de las pestañas. Esfumar la línea negra formando una V, enfatizando el borde externo y elevándola visualmente, dejar la línea inferior libre. **8.** Acentuar el párpado superior móvil con sombra para ojos en polvo blanco perlado. **9.** Aplicar a las pestañas una máscara que agregue volumen. **10.** Aplicar a las mejillas rubor rosa pálido. Para finalizar el maquillaje utilizar un lápiz labial rosa pálido.

1

2

3

4

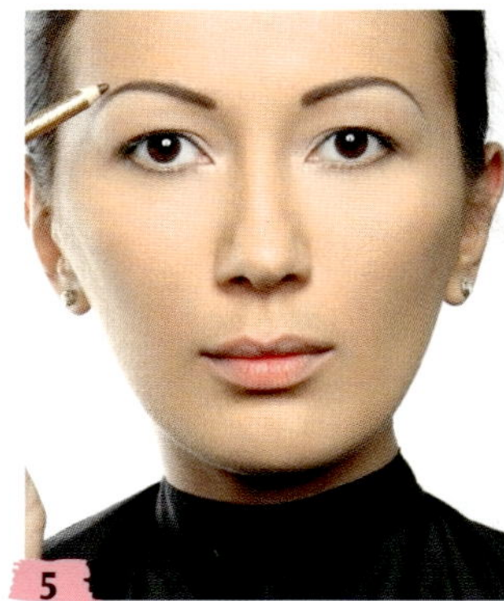
5

6

7

8

9

10

Model: Anna Krupenina

HOT CHOCOLATE

ENGLISH

1. Mask problem skin areas with a concealer that is a tone lighter than the natural skin color. Even the skin tone with powder of natural shade. **2.** Apply brown matte shadow to the upper and lower eyelids. **3.** Accentuate the outer eye corner with black shadow to round the eyelid visually. **4.** Accentuate the natural eyebrow line with a taupe pencil, style the eyebrows with transparent gel in the proper direction. **5.** Apply black lengthening mascara to the upper eyelashes, color the lower lashes with golden mascara. **6.** Refresh the face with subtle peach-like rouge. **7.** To finish the look, apply a pale beige lip color to the lips.

FRANÇAIS

1. Camouflez les zones à imperfections du visage avec un correcteur un peu plus clair que la couleur de la peau. Pour unifier le teint du visage, utilisez une poudre de couleur naturelle. **2.** Appliquez des ombres mates brunes sur les paupières supérieures et inférieures. **3.** Mettez en valeur le coin externe de l'œil, en arrondissant visuellement la paupière. **4.** Marquez le contour des sourcils avec un crayon gris-brun en suivant leur ligne naturelle, gainez-les au gel capillaire incolore pour les discipliner. **5.** Utilisez un mascara noir effet volume pour les cils supérieurs, et un mascara doré pour les cils inférieurs.
6. Rehaussez l'éclat du visage avec des fards à joues avec une couleur douce de pêche.
7. Pour terminer le maquillage, mettez un rouge à lèvres beige pâle.

DEUTSCH

1. Kaschieren Sie Problemzonen mit einem Concealer, der eine Nuance heller ist, als Ihr Hautton. Einen ebenmäßigen Teint erhalten Sie mit einem Puder in einem natürlichen Farbton. **2.** Tragen Sie einen matten braunen Lidschatten auf die Ober- und Unterlider auf. **3.** Betonen Sie den äußeren Augenwinkel mit einem schwarzen Lidschatten, um das Augenlid optisch runder wirken zu lassen. **4.** Ziehen Sie die natürliche Augenbrauenform mit einem graubraunen Stift nach. Bringen Sie die Augenbrauen mit einem transparenten Gel in Form. **5.** Tragen Sie eine schwarze, wimpernverlängernde Mascara auf die oberen Wimpern auf. Verwenden Sie goldfarbene Mascara für den unteren Wimpernkranz. **6.** Verwenden Sie ein dezentes, pfirsichfarbenes Rouge für einen frischen Look. **7.** Vervollständigen Sie das Make-up mit einem blassen, beigefarbenen Lippenstift.

ESPAÑOL

1. Ocultar las áreas problemáticas con un corrector de un tono menor que el de la piel. Emparejar el tono de la piel con polvo de una gama natural. **2.** Aplicar sombra marrón mate en los párpados superior e inferior. **3.** Acentuar el borde externo con sombra negra para darle una apariencia redondeada al párpado.
4. Resaltar la línea natural de las cejas con lápiz marrón topo, diseñar las cejas con gel transparente siguiendo la dirección adecuada. **5.** Aplicar una máscara alargadora a las pestañas superiores, pintar las pestañas inferiores con una máscara dorada. **6.** Dar frescura al rostro con un rouge símil durazno.
7. Para finalizar el maquillaje, aplicar un labial de color beige pálido.

1

2

3

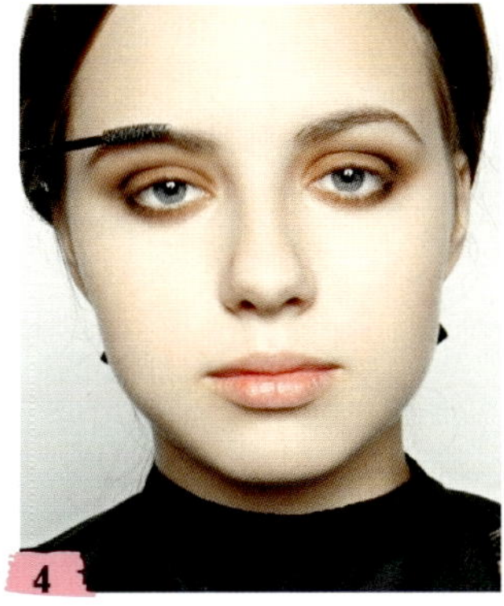
4

5

6

7

Model: Darya Smirnova

MIAMI SUMMER

ENGLISH

1. Mask the problem areas of the face with concealer of natural color, a little lighter than the skin tone. **2.** Even the skin tone with bronzing foundation spray. **3.** Apply white pearl cream shadow to the inner eye corner and under the eyebrow to accentuate the volume of the eyelid. **4.** Apply dark golden cream shadow to the outer corner of the eye spreading it to the lower and upper eyelid. **5.** Define brows with a taupe pencil correcting their natural shape. **6.** Contour the eyes with a dark brown from inside and outside, slightly smudging the contour with dark brown golden shadow. **7.** Apply black volumizing mascara to the eyelashes. **8.** Refresh the face with peach-like light reflecting blusher. **9.** Accentuate the natural shape of the lips with a moisturizing lipstick of a natural beige shade.

FRANÇAIS

1. A l'aide d'un correcteur de teint naturel légèrement plus clair que la couleur de la peau, corrigez les défauts du visage. **2.** Pour unifier le teint du visage, utilisez un fond de teint en spray effet bronzant. **3.** Etalez des ombres à paupières en crème blanc nacré dans le coin interne de l'œil et sur l'arcade sourcilière en soulignant l'arrondi de la paupière. **4.** Appliquez des ombres à paupières en crème doré foncé dans le coin externe, étendez-les sur les paupières inférieures et supérieures. **5.** Soulignez le contour des sourcils à l'aide d'un crayon gris-beige en corrigeant sa forme. **6.** Dessinez un trait le long des cils et suivant le contour à l'intérieur de l'œil avec un crayon brun foncé. Estompez le trait avec des ombres à paupières de couleur brun foncé aux reflets dorés. **7.** Mettez un mascara noir effet volume sur les cils. **8.** Rafraîchissez le visage à l'aide d'un fond de teint couleur pêche avec des particules réflectrices de lumière. **9.** Soulignez la forme des lèvres avec un rouge à lèvres de couleur naturelle beige.

DEUTSCH

1. Kaschieren Sie die Problemzonen im Gesicht mit einem Concealer, der eine Nuance heller ist, als Ihr Hautton. **2.** Verwenden Sie ein Bronzing-Foundation-Spray für einen ebenmäßigen Teint. **3.** Tragen Sie einen perlmuttweißen Cremelidschatten auf den inneren Augenwinkel und unterhalb der Augenbraue auf, um das Volumen des Augenlids zu betonen. **4.** Tragen Sie einen dunklen goldfarbenen Cremelidschatten im äußeren Augenwinkel. auf und verwischen Sie diesen zum Ober- und Unterlid hin. **5.** Ziehen Sie die natürliche Augenbrauenform mit einem graubraunen Augenbrauenstift nach. **6.** Ziehen Sie die Augenkontur in einem dunklen Braunton, innen und außen, nach. Verwischen Sie die Kontur mit einem dunkelbraunen, goldenen Lidschatten. **7.**Tragen Sie Volumen-Mascara auf. **8.** Ein pfirsichfarbenes, lichtreflektierendes Rouge verleiht dem Gesicht Frische. **9.** Betonen Sie die natürliche Lippenform mit einem feuchtigkeitsspendenden Lippenstift in einem natürlichen Beigeton.

ESPAÑOL

1. Ocultar las áreas problemáticas del rostro con un corrector de color natural, un tono menor que el de la piel. **2.** Emparejar el tono de la piel con una base bronceadora atomizada. **3.** Aplicar sombra en crema de color blanco nacarado en el borde interno y debajo de las cejas para acentuar el volumen del párpado.
4. Aplicar sombra en crema de color dorado oscuro en el borde externo del ojo esparciéndola hacia los párpados superiores e inferiores.
5. Definir las cejas con lápiz marrón topo, corrigiendo su forma natural.
6. Dar marco a los ojos con un marrón oscuro desde adentro y afuera, esfumando el contorno con una sombra castaño dorado oscuro.
7.Aplicar a las pestañas una máscara que agregue volumen de color negro.
8. Dar frescura al rostro con un rubor luminoso en tono de durazno.
9. Acentuar la forma natural de los labios con un lápiz labial humectante en un tono beige natural.

1

2

3

4

5

6

7

8

9

Model: Elizaveta Kashirina

GREAT GAME

ENGLISH

1. Even the skin tone and mask small problems of the skin with matte foundation. **2.** To make the skin tone more natural use semitransparent powder. **3.** Accentuate the inner eye corner and upper movable lid with white shadow. Apply it under the eyebrow lifting up the eyebrow end visually. **4.** Accentuate the outer eye corner brightly with matte brown shadow. Smudge the shadow to the lower eyelid and the crease of the upper lid to get a V-shape. **5.** Draw an arrow with black shadow on the upper eyelid starting from the middle of the eye. Smudge the black shadow to get a V-shape, too, accentuating the outer eye corner and lifting it up visually. **6.** Accentuate the natural eyebrow shape with a taupe pencil. **7.** Color the eyelashes with black lengthening mascara. **8.** Apply suntan blusher to correct the facial contours. **9.** Use a pencil of natural color for the lip contour. Contour the lips rounding out their shape. **10.** To finish, use a light beige lipstick.

FRANÇAIS

1. Dissimulez les zones à imperfections du visage avec un correcteur de couleur légèrement plus claire que celle de la carnation de la peau. **2.** Pour donner un aspect naturel, utilisez une poudre semi-transparente. **3.** Accentuez le coin interne de l'œil et la paupière mobile supérieure avec des ombres à paupières blanches. Appliquez-les également sur l'arcade sourcilière, ce qui soulèvera visuellement la pointe des sourcils. **4.** Renforcez le coin externe de l'œil en mettant des ombres à paupières mates brunes. Estompez les ombres sur la paupière inférieure et dans le pli palpébral pour obtenir un angle plus soutenu formant la lettre « V ». **5.** Faites un trait d'eyeliner au ras des cils supérieurs à partir du milieu de l'œil avec des ombres à paupières noires. Estompez les ombres de la même manière en forme de lettre « V » en renforçant le coin externe de l'œil et en le relevant visuellement. **6.** Marquez le contour des sourcils avec un crayon gris-brun en suivant leur ligne naturelle. **7.** Pour les cils utilisez un mascara noir effet volume. **8.** Etalez des fards à paupières effet bronzé en dégageant l'ovale du visage. **9.** Travaillez avec un crayon à lèvres de couleur naturelle. Marquez le contour des lèvres en arrondissant leur forme. **10.** Pour terminer le maquillage, appliquez un rouge à lèvres beige clair.

DEUTSCH

1. Kaschieren Sie kleine Unregelmäßigkeiten mit einer matten Foundation, um einen ebenmäßigen Teint zu erhalten. **2.** Verwenden Sie einen halbtransparentenPuder für einen natürlicheren Teint. **3.** Betonen Sie den inneren Augenwinkel und das bewegliche Oberlid mit weißem Lidschatten. Tragen Sie diesen unterhalb der Augenbraue auf, um diese optisch zu heben. **4.** Betonen Sie den äußeren Augenwinkel mit einem matten braunen Lidschatten. Verwischen Sie den Lidschatten zum unteren Augenlid und zur oberen Lidfalte hin, um eine V-Form zu erhalten. **5.** Gestalten Sie mit einem schwarzen Lidschatten einen schwarzen Pfeil auf das Oberlid. Startpunkt ist die Augenmitte. Verwischen Sie den schwarzen Lidschatten, um eine V-Form zu erhalten. Das betont den äußeren Augenwinkel und hebt diesen optisch an. **6.** Betonen Sie die natürliche Augenbrauenform mit einem graubraunen Stift. **7.** Tragen Sie schwarze, wimpernverlängernde Mascara auf. **8.** Tragen Sie einen sonnengebräunten Rougeton auf, um die Gesichtskonturen zu korrigieren. **9.** Ziehen Sie die Lippen in einer natürlichen Farbe nach. Gestalten Sie diese optisch runder. **10.** Vervollständigen Sie den Look mit einem hellen, beigefarbenen Lippenstift.

ESPAÑOL

1. Emparejar el tono de la piel y ocultar los pequeños problemas de la piel con una base mate. **2.** Para que el tono de la piel sea más natural utilizar polvo semitransparente. **3.** Acentuar el borde interno del ojo y el párpado superior móvil con sombra blanca. Aplicarla debajo de las cejas elevando visualmente sus extremos. **4.** Acentuar el borde externo del ojo intensamente con una sombra marrón mate. Esfumarla hacia el párpado inferior y el pliegue del párpado superior para obtener una forma en V. **5.** Trazar una flecha con sombra negra en el párpado superior comenzado en el medio del ojo. Esfumar la sombra negra para obtener, también, una forma en V; así se acentúa el borde externo del ojo y lo eleva visualmente. **6.** Acentuar la forma natural de las cejas mediante un lápiz de color marrón topo. **7.** Aplicar una máscara que alargue las pestañas de color negro. **8.** Aplicar polvo bronceador para corregir el contorno facial. **9.** Utilizar un lápiz de color natural para el contorno de los labios. Contornear los labios rellenado su forma. **10.** Para finalizar, utilizar un lápiz labial beige claro.

1

2

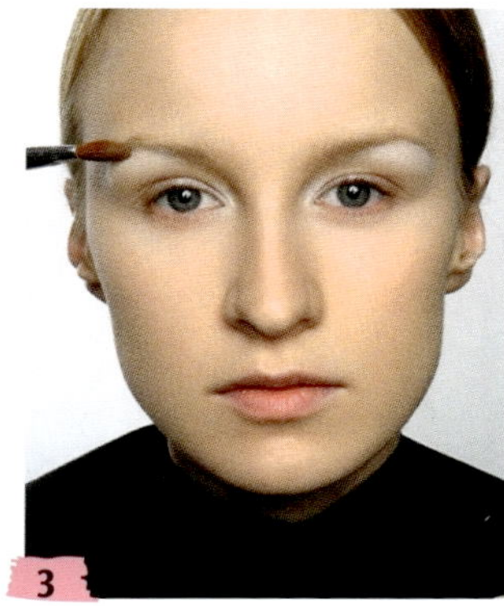
3

4

5

6

7

8

9

10

Model: Maria Buchanenko

CLEAR LINE

ENGLISH

1. Mask the problem areas of the face with concealer of natural color, a little lighter than the skin tone. **2.** To even the complexion, apply matte makeup foundation, avoiding the T-zone and areas under the eyes if possible. **3.** Use a matte powder of natural color to blend the concealer and foundation for a fresh, smooth complexion. **4.** Draw the eyebrows with a light grey and beige pencil, accentuating their natural shape.
5. Apply white pearl cream shadow to the inner eye corner and under the eyebrow to make eyes more voluminous. **6.** Apply brown and brick shadow to the upper eye lid to the crease accentuating the outer eye corner.
7. Blend the shadows with a pale pink powder shade, apply a small amount of pale pink shade to the outer corner of the upper eyelid.
8. Accentuate the eyelash line on the upper lid with black matte shadow, laying emphasis on the outer eye corner, and blend. **9.** Color the eyelashes with lengthening mascara. **10.** To finish, apply shimmery semi-transparent gloss to the lips.

FRANÇAIS

1. Dissimulez les zones à imperfections du visage avec un correcteur de couleur légèrement plus claire que celle de la carnation de la peau.
2. Pour donner à la peau un aspect lisse, appliquez un fond de teint matifiant, en évitant la zone T et la région sous les yeux. **3.** Balayez le visage avec une poudre libre de couleur identique à la carnation pour le rafraichir et estompez les différences entre le correcteur et le fond de teint.
4. Marquez le contour des sourcils avec un crayon gris-brun en suivant leur ligne naturelle. **5.** Etalez des ombres à paupières en crème de couleur blanc nacré dans le coin interne de l'œil et sur l'arcade sourcilière en soulignant l'arrondi de la paupière. **6.** Appliquez des ombres à paupières brun rouge sur le pli palpébral en laissant l'angle externe plus soutenu que celui de l'intérieur de l'œil. **7.** Estompez bien des ombres à paupières rose pâle en poudre pour faire disparaître la limite des ombres précédentes et appliquez-les dans le coin externe des paupières supérieures. **8.** Marquez le contour de la paupière supérieur au ras des cils avec des ombres à paupières noires mates en les étendant bien et en les estompant afin d'intensifier davantage le coin externe de l'œil. **9.** Gainez à l'aide un mascara noir effet volume sur les cils. **10.** Pour terminer ce maquillage, appliquez un brillant semi-transparent irisé sur les lèvres.

DEUTSCH

1. Kaschieren Sie die Problemzonen Ihres Gesichts mit einem Concealer in einer natürlichen Farbe, der eine Nuance heller ist als Ihr Teint.
2. Verwenden Sie eine matte Foundation, um einen ebenmäßigen Teint zu erhalten. Vermeiden Sie die T-Zone und den Bereich um die Augen. **3.** Verwenden Sie matten, natürlichen Puder, um den Concealer und die Foundation zu einem frischen, glatten Look zu verbinden.
4. Ziehen Sie die Augenbrauen mit einem hellgrauen und beigefarbenen Augenbrauenstift nach. **5.** Tragen Sie einen weißenCreme-Lidschatten mit Perlmuttschimmer auf den inneren Augenwinkel und unterhalb der Augenbraue auf, um die Augen größer wirken zu lassen. **6.** Tragen Sie einen braunen und ziegelroten Lidschatten auf das obere Augenlid bis zur Lidfalte auf, um den äußeren Augenwinkel zu betonen. **7.** Verwischen Sie die Lidschattenfarben mit einem blass-pinken Puder-Lidschatten. **8.** Betonen Sie den oberen Wimpernrand mit einem schwarzen, matten Lidschatten. Betonen Sie den äußeren Augenwinkel und verwischen Sie das Ganze. **9.** Betonen Sie die Wimpern mit wimpernverlängernder Mascara. **10.** Verblenden Sie die Lidschatten mit einem blassrosa Ton und tragen Sie etwas blassroa Lidschatten auf den Außenwinkel des oberen Augenlids auf.

ESPAÑOL

1. Ocultar las áreas problemáticas de la cara con corrector de color natural, un tono menor que el de la piel.
2. Para emparejar el rostro, aplicar base para maquillaje mate evitando, de ser posible, la zona de la T y bajo los ojos. **3.** Utilizar polvo mate de color natural para combinar el corrector con la base y lograr un cutis más fresco y suave. **4.** Dibujar las cejas con un lápiz gris claro y beige, acentuando su forma natural. **5.** Aplicar sombra en crema de color blanco perlado en el borde interno del ojo y debajo de la ceja para lograr un ojo más grande. **6.** Aplicar sombra marrón y ladrillo en el párpado superior hasta el pliegue, acentuando el borde exterior del ojo. **7.** Unir los tonos con una sombra rosada clara. Aplicar una pequeña cantidad de esta sombra al borde externo del párpado superior. **8.** Destacar la línea de las pestañas del párpado superior con una sombra negra mate, acentuando el borde exterior del ojo y fundir. **9.** Pintar las pestañas con una máscara para alargar. **10.** Para finalizar, aplicar brillo reluciente semi-transparente en los labios.

Model: Elena Belousova

NATURAL LOOK IS ONE OF THE MOST NOTICEABLE TRENDS IN THE MODERN MAKE-UP. IN THE FOLLOWING PAGES, WE WILL REVEAL YOU THE SECRET OF CREATING A "CLEAN", YET PERFECT FACE WITH A NATURAL PALETTE OF COLORS.

LE STYLE NATUREL, C'EST UNE DES TENDANCES LES PLUS REMARQUABLES DU MAQUILLAGE CONTEMPORAIN. DANS LES PAGES QUI SUIVENT, NOUS VOUS OUVRONS LES SECRETS D'UNE CRÉATION « PURE », TOUT EN GARDANT UN VISAGE PARFAIT À L'AIDE DE TEINTES DE LA PALETTE DES TONS NATURELS.

EIN NATÜRLICHER LOOK IST EINER DER BELIEBTESTEN TRENDS IN DER MODERNEN MAKE-UP-WELT. AUF DEN FOLGENDEN SEITEN VERRATEN WIR IHNEN DAS GEHEIMNIS EINES"NATÜRLICHEN", JEDOCH PERFEKTEN LOOKS MIT NATÜRLICHEN FARBEN.

EL ESTILO NATURAL ES UNA DE LAS TENDENCIAS MÁS VISIBLES EN EL MAQUILLAJE MODERNO. EN LAS PRÓXIMAS PÁGINAS LES REVELAREMOS LOS SECRETOS PARA LOGRAR UNA CARA DESPOJADA Y SIN EMBRAGO, PERFECTA CON UNA PALETA DE COLORES NATURALES.

SUN SHORE

ENGLISH

1. Apply light reflecting foundation to the face. **2.** Even the complexion with a concealer close to the skin tone. **3.** To make the face radiant use slightly glossy semitransparent powder. **4.** Apply light golden crisp shadow to the upper and lower eyelids. **5.** Apply copper crisp shadow to the crease of the upper lid to round out the eye visually. Smudge the shadow thoroughly. **6.** Style the eyebrows with transparent gel accentuating their natural shape. **7.** Color the eyelashes with black mascara. **8.** Refresh the skin tone with slightly radiant coral and pink blusher. **9.** Apply semitransparent pale pink gloss the lips.

FRANÇAIS

1. Commencez par l'application d'une base de maquillage à fines particules réflectrices de lumière sur le visage. **2.** Pour unifier le teint du visage, utilisez un fond de teint de couleur naturelle. **3.** Utilisez une poudre semi-transparente au léger brillant pour apporter de la luminosité au visage. **4.** Etalez des ombres à paupières en poudre de couleur claire et dorée sur les paupières supérieures et inférieures. **5.** Etalez des ombres à paupières couleur bronze dans le pli palpébral de la paupière supérieure en arrondissant visuellement l'œil. Estompez bien les ombres. **6.** Appliquez les sourcils avec un gel capillaire incolore sur les sourcils en gardant leur ligne naturelle. **7.** Utilisez un mascara noir pour les cils. **8.** Rehaussez l'éclat du visage avec des fards à joues rose aux reflets légers. **9.** Mettez un blush semi-transparent rose clair sur les lèvres.

DEUTSCH

1. Tragen Sie eine lichtreflektierende Foundation auf. **2.** Verwenden Sie einen Concealer, der eine Nuance heller ist, als Ihr Hautton, um einen ebenmäßigen Teint zu erhalten. **3.** Verwenden Sie einen halb-transparenten, schimmernden Puder. **4.** Tragen Sie einen hellen, frischen goldenen Lidschatten auf die Ober- und Unterlider auf. **5.** Tragen Sie einen frischen Lidschatten in einem Kupferton auf die Oberlidfalte auf, um das Auge optisch runder zu gestalten. Verwischen Sie den Lidschatten gründlich. **6.** Bringen Sie die Augenbrauen mit einem transparenten Gel in ihre natürliche Form. **7.** Betonen Sie die Augen mit schwarzer Mascara. **8.** Ein strahlendes korallrotes- und rosafarbenes Rouge verleiht Ihrem Teint Frische. **9.** Tragen Sie halbtransparentes, hellrosa Lipgloss auf.

ESPAÑOL

1. Aplicar una base luminosa en la cara. **2.** Emparejar el cutis con un corrector de un tono semejante al de la piel. **3.** Para que se vea radiante, utilizar polvo semitransparente apenas brilloso. **4.** Aplicar sombra compacta de color dorado en los párpados inferiores y superiores. **5.** Aplicar sombra compacta color cobrizo al pliegue del párpado superior hasta rellenar el ojo visualmente. Esfumar la sombra completamente. **6.** Diseñar las cejas con gel transparente, acentuando su forma natural. **7.** Pintar las pestañas con máscara negra. **8.** Refrescar el tono de la piel con un rubor apenas brilloso de color coral y rosa. **9.** Aplicar brillo semitransparente color rosa pálido a los labios.

Model: Zhanna Danilova

WIND ROSE

ENGLISH

1. To even the complexion, apply light reflecting foundation close to skin tone. **2.** Sweep a pale pink shade under brow and over lid. **3.** To intensify the color, sweep a sheer mineral shadow in a copper tone under the brow and over the lid. **4.** Contour the eyes with dark brown eyeliner **5.** Applying mascara to the eyelashes thoroughly. **6.** To make the complexion more fresh, use whity-pink golden blusher. **7.** As a finishing touch, apply pale pink lip gloss.

FRANÇAIS

1. Unifiez le teint du visage en appliquant sur le visage un fond de teint à fines particules réflectrices de lumière de couleur identique à la carnation. **2.** Appliquez des ombres à paupières rose pâle nacrées sur l'arcade sourcilière. **3.** Intensifiez le maquillage avec des ombres à paupières de couleur bronze en les appliquant sur les paupières mobiles inférieures et supérieures et en les estompant minutieusement. **4.** Dessinez un trait léger sur tout le contour de l'œil à l'aide d'un crayon brun foncé. **5.** Appliquez soigneusement un mascara effet volume. **6.** Rehaussez l'éclat du visage avec un blush irisé rose clair. **7.** Pour terminer le maquillage, mettez un brillant rose pâle.

DEUTSCH

1. Tragen Sie eine lichtreflektierende Foundation in Ihrem Hautton auf, um einen ebenmäßigen Teint zu erhalten. **2.** Tragen Sie einen blass-pinken Lidschatten unterhalb der Augenbraue und über das gesamte Augenlid auf. **3.** Um die Farbe zu verstärken, tragen Sie einen hellen Mineral-Lidschatten in einem Kupferton unterhalb der Augenbraue und auf das Augenlid auf. **4.** Betonen Sie die Augen mit einem dunkelbraunen Eyeliner. **5.** Tragen Sie ausreichend Mascara auf. **6.** Tragen Sie einen weiß-pinkenRougeton mit leichten Goldtönen auf die Wangenknochen auf, um einen frischen Teint zu erhalten. **7.** Vervollständigen Sie den Look mit einem blass-pinken Lipgloss.

ESPAÑOL

1. Para emparejar el tono del cutis, aplicar base luminosa de un color cercano al de la piel. **2.** Aplicar con un pincel un tono rosa pálido debajo de la ceja y sobre el párpado. **3.** Para intensificar el color aplicar con un pincel una sombra en tono cobrizo, debajo de las cejas y sobre el párpado. **4.** Contornear los ojos con un delineador marrón oscuro. **5.** Enmascarando completamente las pestañas. **6.** Para dar frescura al cutis, usar un rubor dorado con una pizca de rosa. **7.** Como toque final, aplicar un brillo labial en un tono rosa pálido.

1

2

3

4

5

6

7

Model: Alyona Alyoshina

UNADORNED BEAUTY

ENGLISH

1. Apply light reflecting foundation to the face. **2.** Mask problem skin areas and areas under the eyes with a light concealer. . To even the skin tone use a mattifying concealer. **3.**Apply powder close to the skin tone. Correct the facial contours with darker powder. **4.** Apply white matte shadow under the eyebrow and to the inner eye corner. **5.** Apply beige matte shadow the upper immovable lid to round out the eye visually. **6.** Slightly accentuate the outer eye corner with a dark brown pencil. **7.** Draw the eyebrow line with soft brown shadow. **8.** Color the upper and lower eyelashes with black mascara. **9.** Contour the lips with a lip pencil close to the lip color. **10.** Apply suntan blusher to the cheekbones to make them more expressive. Apply a little slightly radiant gloss to the lips.

FRANÇAIS

1. Appliquez une base de maquillage à fines particules réflectrices de lumière sur le visage. **2.** Appliquez un correcteur de teint clair, pour dissimuler les imperfections du visage et sous les yeux. Pour unifier le teint, utilisez un fond de teint matifiant. **3.** Balayez une poudre de teinte naturelle sur le visage. Corrigez la forme du visage avec une poudre de teinte plus foncée. **4.** Etalez des ombres à paupières mates blanches sur l'arcade sourcilière et dans le coin externe de l'œil. **5.** Mettez des ombres à paupières mates beiges sur la paupière mobile supérieure pour arrondir visuellement l'œil. **6.** Marquez légèrement le coin externe de l'œil avec un crayon brun foncé. **7.** Tracez la ligne du sourcil avec des ombres à paupières de teinte brun fumé. **8.** Posez un mascara noir sur les cils supérieurs et inférieurs. **9.** Faites le contour des lèvres avec un crayon à lèvres de teinte naturelle. **10.** Etalez un blush effet bronzé, pour dégager les pommettes. Mettez un peu de brillant aux reflets veloutés sur les lèvres.

DEUTSCH

1. Tragen Sie eine lichtreflektierende Foundation auf. **2.** Kaschieren Sie Problemzonen und den Bereich unterhalb der Augen mit einem hellen Concealer. Verwenden Sie einen mattierenden Concealer für einen ebenmäßigen Teint. **3.** Tragen Sie einen Puder in Ihrem Hautton auf. Korrigieren Sie die Gesichtskonturen mit einem dunkleren Puder. **4.** Tragen Sie einen weißen, matten Lidschatten unterhalb der Augenbrauen und zum inneren Augenwinkel hin, auf. **5.** Tragen Sie einen beigefarbenen, matten Lidschatten auf das unbewegliche Oberlid auf, um die Augen optisch runder wirken zu lassen. **6.**Betonen Sie den äußeren Augenwinkel leicht mit einem dunkelbraunen Stift. **7.** Ziehen Sie die Augenbrauenlinie mit einem weichen braunen Lidschatten nach. **8.** Tragen Sie schwarze Mascara auf. **9.** Ziehen Sie die Lippen mit einem Konturstift in einer natürlichen Farbe nach. **10.** Tragen Sie ein Rouge in einem sonnengebräunten ton auf die Wangenknochen auf, um diese betonen. Vervollständigen Sie den Look mit einem leicht strahlenden Lipgloss.

ESPAÑOL

1. Aplicar una base luminosa en el rostro. **2.** Ocultar las áreas problemáticas de la piel y las áreas bajo los ojos con un corrector. Para emparejar el tono de la piel usar un corrector mate. **3.** Aplicar polvo de un tono semejante al de la piel. Corregir el contorno del rostro con polvo más oscuro. **4.** Aplicar sombra blanca mate debajo de las cejas y en el borde interno de los ojos. **5.** Aplicar sombra de color beige mate sobre el párpado superior fijo para rellenar visualmente el ojo. **6.** Acentuar delicadamente el borde externo del ojo con lápiz marrón oscuro. **7.** Trazar la línea de las cejas con una sombra marrón claro **8.** Pintar las pestañas superiores e inferiores con máscara negra. **9.** Contornear los labios con un lápiz labial de un color cercano al de los labios. **10.** Aplicar rubor color broceado en los pómulos para hacerlas más expresivas. Aplicar un brillo apenas luminoso sobre los labios.

Model: Anna Krupenina

MISS NATURAL

ENGLISH

1. Apply light reflecting foundation to the face. **2.** To even the skin tone use a concealer with a luminescent effect **3.** To make the face look more natural use slightly radiant semitransparent powder. **4.** Correct the eyebrow shape with taupe shadow. Style the eyebrows with transparent gel in the proper direction. **5.** Apply pale pink shadow to the upper and lower eye lids. **6.** Highlight the upper eyelid with beige shadow accentuating the outer eye corner. **7.** Apply suntan matte blusher to correct the facial contours. Apply a little pale pink pearl blusher to the cheekbones. **8.** Apply a caring lipstick to the lips. Accentuate the natural shape of the lips and color them thoroughly with a lip pencil close to the lip color. **9.** Color only the upper eyelashes with black mascara.

FRANÇAIS

1. Appliquez une base de maquillage à fines particules réflectrices de lumière sur le visage. **2.** Pour unifier le teint, utilisez un fond de teint effet lumineux. **3.** Pour rendre le teint du visage plus naturel, balayez-le avec une poudre semi-transparente légèrement nacrée. **4.** Corrigez la forme des sourcils en appliquant des ombres à paupières gris-brun. Gainez les sourcils avec un gel incolore dans le sens désiré. **5.** Etalez des ombres à paupières rose clair sur les paupières inférieures et supérieures. **6.** Accentuez la paupière supérieure avec des ombres beiges, étalez-les vers le coin externe de l'œil. **7.** Appliquez des fards à joues opaques couleur effet bronzé en corrigeant l'ovale du visage. Passez un peu de fards rose clair nacrés sur les pommettes. **8.** Mettez du baume à lèvres. Mettez en valeur la forme naturelle des lèvres en traçant le contour avec un crayon à lèvres de couleur naturelle. Remplissez aussi les lèvres avec le crayon. **9.** Mettez un mascara noir uniquement sur les cils supérieurs.

DEUTSCH

1. Tragen Sie eine lichtreflektierende Foundation auf. **2.** Verwenden Sie einen lumineszierenden Concealer für einen ebenmäßigen Teint. **3.** Ein leicht strahlender, halb-transparenter Puder verleiht dem Gesicht einen natürlichen Look. **4.** Korrigieren Sie die Augenbrauenform mit einem graubraunen Lidschatten. Bringen Sie die Augenbrauen mit einem transparenten Gel in Form. **5.** Tragen Sie einen hellrosa Lidschatten auf Ober- und Unterlider auf. **6.** Betonen Sie das Oberlid und den äußeren Augenwinkel mit beigefarbenem Lidschatten. **7.** Tragen Sie ein Rouge in einem matten, sonnengebräunten Ton auf, um die Gesichtskonturen hervorzuheben. Tragen Sie einen Hauch blassrosafarbenes Rouge mit Perlmuttglanz auf die Wangenknochen auf. **8.** Verwenden Sie einen pflegenden Lippenstift. Betonen Sie die natürliche Form der Lippen mit einem Lipliner in einer natürlichen Farbe und tragen Sie diesen auf die gesamten Lippen auf. **9.** Betonen Sie ausschließlich den oberen Wimpernkranz mit Mascara.

ESPAÑOL

1. Aplicar una base luminosa en el rostro. **2.** Para emparejar el tono de la piel utilizar un corrector con efecto lumínico. **3.** Para dar una apariencia más natural a la cara, usar polvo semitransparente apenas resplandeciente. **4.** Corregir la forma de la ceja con sombra marrón topo. Diseñar las cejas con gel transparente siguiendo la dirección adecuada. **5.** Aplicar sombra color rosa pálido sobre el párpado superior e inferior. **6.** Resaltar el párpado superior con sombra beige acentuando el borde externo del ojo. **7.** Aplicar rubor mate de tono bronceado para corregir el contorno facial. Aplicar un rubor de color rosa pálido perlado sobre los pómulos. **8.** Aplicar un protector labial sobre los labios. Acentuar la forma natural de los labios y pintarlos completamente con un lápiz labial de un color semejante al de los labios. **9.** Pintar solo las pestañas superiores con máscara negra.

1

2

3

4

5

6

7

8

9

Model: Anna Volkova

MADEMOISELLE BEIGE

ENGLISH

1. Even the complexion with a mattifying concealer close to the skin tone. Correct the facial contours with and nose shape with powder of two shades. **2.** Accentuate the upper movable lid and the area under the eyebrow with white matte shadows. **3.** Apply beige matte shadow to crease of the upper eyelid and the outer corner of the lower lid. Blend the shadow thoroughly. **4.** Accentuate the natural eyebrow line with a taupe pencil, style the eyebrows with transparent gel. **5.** Color the eyelashes with black lengthening mascara. **6.** Apply a matte lipstick of natural pale beige color to the lips. **7.** Refresh the face with bronzing blush.

FRANÇAIS

1. Pour unifier le teint du visage, utilisez un fond de teint matifiant de couleur identique à la carnation. Dégagez l'ovale du visage et la forme du nez avec une poudre à deux teintes. **2.** Eclaircissez la paupière mobile supérieure avec des ombres à paupières mates blanches, appliquez-les également sur l'arcade sourcilière. **3.** Etalez des ombres à paupières mates beiges dans le pli palpébral de la paupière supérieure et le coin externe de la paupière inférieure. Estompez bien la limite des ombres. **4.** Soulignez le contour naturel des sourcils avec un crayon gris-brun, dirigez-les dans le sens souhaité en appliquant un gel incolore capillaire pour sourcils. **5.** Pour les cils, prenez un mascara noir allongeant. **6.** Mettez un rouge à lèvres mat de couleur naturelle beige pâle. **7.** Balayez les joues avec un blush effet bronzant pour redonner de l'éclat au visage.

DEUTSCH

1. Verwenden Sie einen mattierenden Concealer für einen ebenmäßigen Teint. Korrigieren Sie die Gesichtskonturen und Nasenform mit Pudern in zwei Farbtönen. **2.** Betonen Sie das bewegliche Oberlid und den Bereich unterhalb der Augenbrauen mit einem weißen, matten Lidschatten. **3.** Tragen Sie einen beigefarbenen, matten Lidschatten in die Oberlidfalte und den äußeren Augenwinkel des Unterlids auf. Verwischen Sie diesen gründlich. **4.** Betonen Sie die natürliche Augenbrauenform mit einem graubraunen Stift. Bringen Sie die Augenbrauen mit einem transparenten Gel in Form. **5.** Tragen Sie eine wimpernverlängernde, schwarze Mascara auf. **6.** Tragen Sie einen matten Lippenstift in einem natürlichen Beigeton auf. **7.** Ein Bronzing Rouge verleiht dem Look die nötige Frische.

ESPAÑOL

1. Emparejar el cutis con corrector mate de un tono cercano al de la piel. Corregir el contorno facial y la forma de la nariz con polvo de dos tonos. **2.** Acentuar el párpado superior móvil y el área bajo la ceja con sombra blanca mate. **3.** Aplicar sombra beige mate al pliegue del párpado superior y al borde externo del párpado inferior. Fundir las sombras completamente. **4.** Acentuar la línea natural de la ceja con lápiz marrón topo, diseñar la ceja con gel transparente. **5.** Pintar las pestañas con máscara prolongadora negra. **6.** Aplicar lápiz labial mate de un tono beige claro natural sobre los labios. **7.** Dar frescura a la cara con un rubor en un tono bronceado.

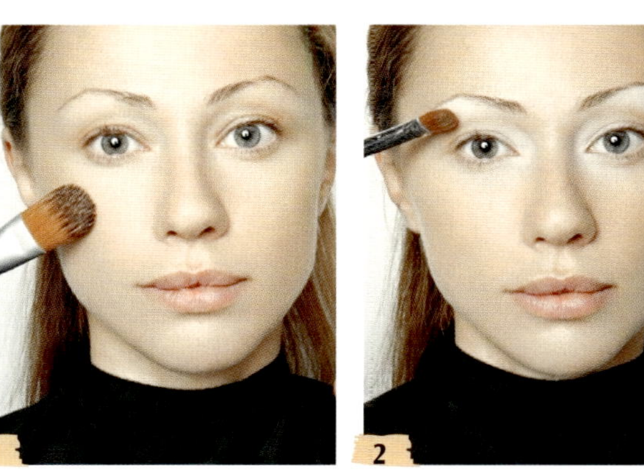

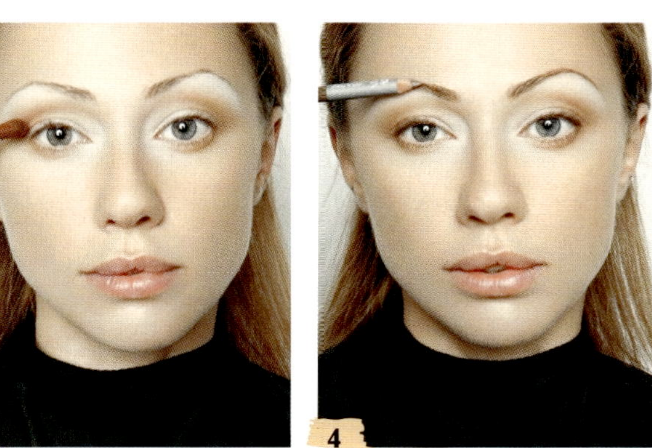

Model: Lika Pimenova

CARAMEL

ENGLISH
1. Even the skin tone and mask small problems of the skin with a mattifying concealer. **2.** Make the skin tone more natural with light reflecting powder. **3.** Style the eyebrows with transparent gel to give them well-groomed appearance. **4.** Apply peach-like creamy blusher with a finger. Apply it as shadow to the upper and lower eyelid in the same way. **5.** Color the eyelashes with black lengthening mascara. **6.** As a finishing touch, apply bright lightcoral gloss to the lips.

FRANÇAIS
1. Pour unifier le teint du visage et camoufler les légères imperfections du visage, utilisez un fond de teint matifiant. **2.** Pour rendre au visage un teint plus naturel, balayez-le avec une poudre à fines particules réflectrices de lumière. **3.** Arrangez les sourcils avec un gel incolore capillaire pour sourcils pour leur donner un aspect plus ordonné. **4.** Etalez au doigt des fards à joues en crème de couleur pêche, utilisez-les également en tant qu'ombres à paupières sur les paupières supérieures et inférieures. **5.** Pour les cils, prenez un mascara noir volumateur. **6.** Pour finir, mettez un gloss de nuance corail clair sur les lèvres.

DEUTSCH
1. Ein mattierender Concealer schafft einen ebenmäßigen Teint und kaschiert Unregelmäßigkeiten. **2.**Ein lichtreflektierender Puder schafft einen natürlichen Teint. **3.** Bringen Sie die Augenbrauen mit einem transparenten Gel in Form und verleihen Sie ihnen so ein gepflegtes Aussehen. **4.** Tragen Sie ein pfirsichfarbenes, cremiges Rouge mit den Fingern auf. Tragen Sie dies auf die gleiche Art und Weise auf Ober- und Unterlid auf. **5.** Verwenden Sie schwarze, wimpernverlängernde Mascara. **6.** Vervollständigen Sie den Look mit einem hellen korallroten Lipgloss.

ESPAÑOL
1. Emparejar el tono de la piel y ocultar los problemas de la piel con un corrector mate. **2.** Dar una apariencia natural a la piel con una base luminosa en polvo. **3.** Trabajar las cejas con un gel transparente para darles una apariencia bien peinada. **4.** Aplicar rubor cremoso color durazno con los dedos. Aplicarlo como sombra en los párpados superiores e inferiores de la misma manera. **5.** Pintar las pestañas con máscara para alargar negra. **6.** Como toque final, aplicar un brillo coral luminoso en los labios.

1

2

3

4

5

6

Model: Anastasiya Papenkova

TO BE STYLISH MEANS NOT JUST TO KEEP UP TO LATEST FASHION TRENDS, BUT TO HAVE ONE'S OWN "HANDWRITING" IN CLOTHES AND MAKE-UP. IMAGES OF THIS SECTION ARE CERTAIN TO SUGGEST YOU A LOT OF INTERESTING SOLUTIONS.

AVOIR DU STYLE, C'EST METTRE EN AVANT SA PROPRE « MARQUE » DANS SON LOOK VESTIMENTAIRE ET SON MAQUILLAGE, ET NON PAS SEULEMENT ÊTRE AU FAIT DES DERNIÈRES TENDANCES DE LA MODE. LES EXEMPLES PRÉSENTÉS DANS CETTE SECTION VOUS GUIDERONT SANS AUCUN DOUTE VERS DES PISTES INTÉRESSANTES.

STYLE BEDEUTET NICHT NUR, MODISCH AUF DEM LAUFENDEN ZU SEIN. ES BEDEUTET AUCH, SEINEN EIGENEN STIL IM BEREICH MODE UND MAKE-UP ZU HABEN. DIE BILDER DIESES ABSCHNITTS SIND VOLLER INTERESSANTER IDEEN.

TENER ESTILO SIGNIFICA, NO SOLO ESTAR AL DÍA CON LAS ÚLTIMAS TENDENCIAS DE LA MODA, SINO TENER TU PROPIO SELLO. EN ROPA Y MAQUILLAJE. ES UN HECHO QUE LAS IMÁGENES DE ESTA SECCIÓN TE SUGERIRÁN MUCHAS SOLUCIONES INTERESANTES.

POP-ROCK

ENGLISH

1. Using a creamy concealer a little lighter than the skin tone, mask problem areas and dark patches under the eyes, accentuate the T-zone, chin and the upper eyelid under the eyebrow line. **2.** Accentuate the alae of the nose, lateral parts of the forehead and the cheekbones with a darker concealer. To make the face matte use translucent mattifying powder. Highlight the natural line of the eyebrows accentuating the ends, and style them with translucent eyebrow gel. **3.** Apply rich black shadow coloring the eyelid crease and accentuating the outer eye corner. **4.** Smudge the border of the black shadow with light brown shadow. Apply light brown shadow to the lower lid to accentuate its volume. Apply pale pink blusher to the cheekbones to refresh the face. **5.** Color the lower eyelashes slightly, apply several layers of lengthening mascara to the upper lashes. Contour the lips with a pencil close to the lip color. **6.** Contour the eyes from inside to make the sight more expressive. Apply a pale beige matte lipstick to the lips.

FRANÇAIS

1. Camouflez les imperfections du visage et les cernes sous les yeux avec un correcteur de teint à texture crème d'une couleur légèrement plus claire que la peau, éclaircissez la « T-zone », le menton et les arcades sourcilières. **2.** Rehaussez les ailes des narines, les parties latérales du front et les pommettes avec un correcteur de teint plus foncé. Pour rendre le visage plus mat, utilisez une poudre transparente matifiante. Tracez les sourcils avec un applicateur pour ombres à paupières avec une couleur beige clair en suivant leur forme naturelle et en accentuant les pointes. Ensuite mettez un gel capillaire incolore pour sourcils. **3.** Appliquez des ombres de couleur noir saturé sur la paupière mobile supérieure, en les étendant bien dans le pli palpébral et en accentuant le coin externe de l'œil. **4.** Estompez la limite des ombres noires avec des ombres brun clair. Ensuite appliquez-les sur la paupière inférieure pour faire ressortir son relief. Balayez les pommettes avec un blush rose pâle pour faire briller la peau. **5.** Appliquez un peu de mascara pour les cils inférieurs et passez plusieurs couches de mascara effet volume sur les cils supérieurs. Marquez le contour des lèvres avec un crayon à lèvres de couleur naturelle. **6.** Faites un trait avec un crayon noir à l'intérieur de l'œil pour intensifier le regard. Mettez un rouge à lèvres mat beige pâle sur les lèvres.

DEUTSCH

1. Verwenden Sie einen cremigen Concealer, der eine Nuance heller ist, als Ihr Hautton, um Problemzonen und dunkle Ringe unter den Augen zu kaschieren. Betonen Sie die T-Zone, das Kinn und Oberlid unterhalb der Augenbraue. **2.** Betonen Sie den Nasenrücken, seitlichen Stirnpartien und Wangenknochen mit einem dunklen Concealer. Mattieren Sie das Gesicht mit einem transparenten, mattierenden Puder. Betonen Sie die natürliche Augenbrauenform durch Betonung der Enden und bringen Sie diese mit einem transparenten Gel in Form. **3.** Tragen Sie einen tiefschwarzen Lidschatten in die Augenlidfalte auf und betonen Sie den äußeren Augenwinkel. **4.** Verwischen Sie den Rand des schwarzen Lidschattens mit einem hellen Braunton. Tragen Sie einen hellbraunen Lidschatten auf das Unterlid auf, um diesem Volumen zu verleihen. Tragen Sie hellrosa Rouge auf die Wangenknochen auf, um einen frischen Look zu erhalten. **5.** Tragen Sie dezent Mascara auf den unteren Wimpernkranz auf und betonen Sie die oberen Wimpern mit mehreren Schichten einer wimpernverlängernden Mascara. Ziehen Sie die Lippenkonturen mit einem Lipliner in ihrer natürlichen Lippenfarbe nach. **6.** Ziehen Sie den inneren Wimpernrand nach, um den Augen Ausdruck zu verleihen. Vervollständigen Sie den Look mit einem beigefarbenen matten Lippenstift.

ESPAÑOL

1. Usando un corrector cremoso de un tono un poco menor que el de la piel, ocultar las áreas problemáticas y las ojeras, acentuar la zona de la T, pera, y el párpado superior bajo la línea de la ceja. **2.** Acentuar las alas de la nariz, los lateral es de la frente, y las mejillas con un corrector más oscuro. Para matizar la cara, utilizar un polvo translúcido mate. Resaltar la línea natural de las cejas acentuando los extremos y modelar con gel translúcido para cejas. **3.** Aplicar sombra de color negro intenso, pintando el pliegue del párpado y destacando el borde exterior del ojo. **4.** Esfumar el borde de la sombra negra con sombra marrón claro. Aplicar sombra de color marrón claro en el párpado inferior para darle más volumen. Aplicar rubor de color rosa pálido a las mejillas para darle más frescura. **5.** Pintar las pestañas inferiores suavemente, aplicar varias capas de de máscara en las pestañas superiores para alargarlas. Contornear los labios con un lápiz de color semejante al de la boca. **6.** Contornear los ojos desde adentro para crear una mirada más expresiva. Aplicar un lápiz labial mate de color beige pálido en los labios.

1

2

3

4

5

6

Model: Ekaterina Ukhanova

COUNTRY STYLE

ENGLISH

1. Even the skin tone and mask small problems of the skin with mattifying foundation. **2.** Make the skin tone more natural with light reflecting powder. **3.** Style the eyebrows with transparent gel to give them a natural shape. **4.** Contour the eye with a black pencil coloring the eyelash line thoroughly. **5.** Smudge the pencil line with brown matte shadow to round out the eye. On the upper eyelid, smudge the pencil line to the brow line. **6.** Color the eyelashes with black lengthening mascara. Apply several layers to get a "spider leg" effect. **7.** Correct the facial contour with light brown matte blusher. **8.** Use a metalescent lipstick close to the lip color.

FRANÇAIS

1. Pour unifier le teint et dissimuler les légères imperfections du visage, utilisez un fond de teint matifiant. **2.** Pour rendre le teint du visage plus naturel, balayez-le avec une poudre à fines particules réflectrices de lumière. **3.** Assagissez les sourcils avec un gel incolore en soulignant leur forme naturelle. **4.** Dessinez un contour net autour de l'œil au ras des cils avec un crayon noir. **5.** Estompez le contour noir avec des ombres à paupières mates brunes pour arrondir l'œil. Etalez les ombres vers les sourcils. **6.** Utilisez un mascara noir effet volume pour les cils. Repassez le mascara plusieurs fois sur les cils, pour créer un effet en « pattes d'araignée ». **7.** Dégager l'ovale du visage à l'aide des fards à joues mats brun clair. **8.** Mettez un rouge à lèvres de teinte naturelle, mais aux reflets cristallins.

DEUTSCH

1. Verwenden Sie einen mattierenden Concealer, um Problemzonen und kleine Unregelmäßigkeiten zu kaschieren. **2.** Ein lichtreflektierender Puder verleiht Ihrer Haut einen natürlichen Look. **3.** Bringen Sie die Augenbrauen mit einem transparenten Gel in ihre natürliche Form. **4.** Ziehen Sie die Augenkonturen mit einem schwarzen Stift nach. Betonen Sie den Wimpernrand. **5.** Verwischen Sie die Linie mit einem braunen, matten Lidschatten, um dem Auge eine runde Form zu verleihen. Verwischen Sie die Linie auf dem Oberlid bis hin zur Augenbraue. **6.** Tragen Sie schwarze, wimpernverlängernde Mascara auf. Tragen Sie mehrere Schichten auf, um den sogenannten „Spinnenbein"-Effekt zu erhalten. **7.** Korrigieren Sie die Gesichtskontur mit einem hellbraunen, matten Rouge. **8.** Verwenden Sie einen Lippenstift mit metalligem Effekt, der ihrer natürlichen Lippenfarbe entspricht.

ESPAÑOL

Emparejar el tono de la piel y ocultar los pequeños problemas de la piel con base mate. **2.** Dar una apariencia más natural a la piel usando polvo luminoso. **3.** Modelar las cejas con gel transparente para darles una forma natural. **4.** Contornear los ojos con un lápiz negro pintando la línea de las pestañas completamente. **5.** Esfumar la línea del lápiz con sombra mate de color marrón para completar el ojo. En el párpado superior, fundir la línea del lápiz con la línea de las cejas. **6.** Pintar las pestañas con una máscara alargadora negra. Aplicar varias capas para lograr un efecto "pestañas postizas". **7.** Corregir el contorno facial. Con rubor mate de color marrón claro. **8.** Utilizar lápiz labial metalizado de un color semejante al de los labios.

1

2

3

4

5

6

7

8

Model: Anastasiya Papenkova

HOT AUTUMN

ENGLISH

1. Mask problem skin areas with a creamy concealer a tone lighter than the natural skin tone. **2.** Even the skin tone with light reflecting concealer. **3.** Highlight the temples, cheekbones and alae of the nose with suntan crisp powder to accentuate the facial features. **4.** Color the upper lid and inner eye corner with light bronze powder. **5.** To accentuate the volume of the eye use dark brown bronze shadow coloring the lower lid and the upper eyelid crease and rounding out the eye. **6.** Accentuate the outer eye corner with black matte shadow.
7. To make the sight clearer contour the eye from the inner side with a black pencil. Color the eyelashes with black mascara thoroughly. **8.** Apply lip gloss of natural color with pearl crumbs to the lips. To finish the make up, apply subtle bronze blusher to the cheekbones.

FRANÇAIS

1. Dissimulez les imperfections du visage avec un correcteur de teint de texture crème d'un ton plus clair que celle de la carnation de la peau.
2. Utilisez un fond de teint matifiant contenant des pigments réflecteurs de lumière pour unifier le teint.
3. A l'aide d'une poudre libre effet bronzant mettez l'accent sur les tempes, les pommettes et les ailes des narines pour mettre en valeur ces traits du visage. **4.** Recouvrez la paupière supérieure et le coin interne de l'œil avec des ombres à paupières en poudre libre de couleur bronzant clair. **5.** Intensifiez le regard en appliquant des ombres à paupières brun foncé à la nuance bronzante sur la paupière inférieure et le pli palpébral de la paupière supérieure, et en arrondissant la forme de l'œil. **6.** Foncez le coin externe avec des ombres noires mates. **7.** Pour rendre le maquillage des yeux plus net, faites un trait avec un crayon noir à l'intérieur de l'œil. Appliquez bien un mascara noir sur les cils.
8. Mettez un gloss de ton naturel aux micro-particules de nacres sur les lèvres. Pour un fini parfait, balayez les pommettes d'un halo d'un blush de couleur bronzante veloutée.

DEUTSCH

1. Verwenden Sie einen cremigen Concealer, der eine Nuance heller ist, als Ihr Hautton, um Problemzonen zu kaschieren. **2.** Ein lichtreflektierender Concealer verleiht Ihnen einen ebenmäßigen Teint. **3.** Betonen Sie die Schläfen, Wangenknochen und den Nasenrücken mit einem frischen Puder mit leichter Sonnenbräune, um die Gesichtskonturen zu betonen.
4. Tragen Sie einen hellen, bronzefarbenen Puder auf das Oberlid und den inneren Augenwinkel auf. **5.** Tragen Sie einen dunkelbraunen, bronzefarbenen Lidschatten auf das untere Lid und die obere Augenlidfalte auf, um das Auge runder wirken zu lassen und diesem Volumen zu verleihen.
6. Betonen Sie den äußeren Augenwinkel mit schwarzem, mattem Lidschatten. **7.** Ziehen Sie die Kontur des Auges am inneren Wimpernrand mit einem schwarzen Stift nach, um einen klaren Blick zu erhalten. Betonen Sie die Wimpern mit ausreichend Mascara. **8.** Tragen Sieein natürliches Lipgloss mit Perlmuttschimmer auf. Vervollständigen Sie den Look durch Auftragen eines bronzefarbenen Rouges auf die Wangenknochen.

ESPAÑOL

1. Ocultar las áreas problemáticas de la piel con un corrector cremoso de un tono menor al de la piel. **2.** Emparejar el tono de la piel con un corrector luminoso. **3.** Destacar las sienes, las mejillas y las alas de la nariz con un polvo radiante color bronceado para acentuar las características del rostro. **4.** Pintar el párpado superior y el borde interno del ojo con polvo bronce claro. **5.** Para acentuar el volumen del ojo utilizar una sombra de color bronce-marrón oscuro, pintando el pliegue del párpado inferior y rellenando el ojo. **6.** Acentuar el borde externo del ojo con sombra mate negra. **7.** Para crear una mirada más clara, contornear el ojo desde el lado interno con lápiz negro. Pintar completamente las pestañas con máscara negra. **8.** Aplicar brillo de color natural con destellos perlados en los labios. Para finalizar el maquillaje, aplicar rubor bronce tenue a los pómulos.

Model: Tatyana Valik

NEODECADENCE

ENGLISH

1. Even the skin tone with light reflecting foundation. **2.** Correct the facial contours with suntan powder. **3.** Apply black matte shadow to the upper and lower movable lids.
4. Smudge the black shadow with shadow of natural brown color. **5.** Accentuate the natural eyebrow line with a taupe pencil, style the eyebrows with transparent gel in the proper direction. Color the eyelashes with black lengthening mascara. **6.** To finish the makeup, apply a light beige lip color to the lips.

FRANÇAIS

1. Pour unifier le teint du visage, utilisez un fond de teint matifiant contenant des pigments réflecteurs de lumière. **2.** Corrigez l'ovale du visage avec une poudre à effet bronzant. **3.** Appliquez des ombres à paupières noires mates sur les paupières inférieures et supérieures. **4.** Estompez les ombres noires en les mélangeant avec des ombres de couleur naturelle brune. **5.** Soulignez le contour naturel des sourcils avec un crayon gris-brun, dirigez-les dans le sens souhaité avec un gel incolore pour sourcils. Pour les cils, utilisez un mascara noir allongeant.
6. Finalisez le maquillage en appliquant un rouge à lèvres de ton beige clair.

DEUTSCH

1. Eine lichtreflektierende Foundation verleiht Ihnen einen ebenmäßigen Teint. **2.** Korrigieren Sie die Gesichtkonturen mit einem Puder mit leichter Sonnenbräune. **3.** Tragen Sie einen schwarzen, matten Lidschatten auf Ober- und Unterlid auf. **4.** Verwischen Sie den schwarzen Lidschatten mit einem Lidschatten in einem natürlichen Braunton. **5.** Betonen Sie die natürliche Augenbrauenform mit einem graubraunen Stift. Bringen Sie die Augenbrauen mit einem transparenten Gel in Form. Tragen Sie eine wimpernverlängernde, schwarze Mascara auf. **6.** Vervollständigen Sie den Look mit einem hellen, beigefarbenen Lippenstift.

ESPAÑOL

1. Emparejar el tono de la piel con base luminosa. **2.** Corregir el contorno facial con polvo de color bronceado. **3.** Aplicar sombra mate negra al párpado superior e inferior móvil.
4. Esfumar la sombra negra con una sombra de un color marrón natural. **5.** Acentuar la línea natural de la ceja con lápiz marrón topo, modelar las cejas con gel transparente en la dirección adecuada. Pintar las pestañas con máscara alargadora negra. **6.** Para finalizar el maquillaje, aplicar labial beige claro a los labios.

1

2

3

4

5

6

Model: Elizaveta Kashirina

ELEGANCE

ENGLISH

1. Even the complexion with mattifying foundation close to the skin tone. **2.** Accentuate the eyebrows with light beige shadow correcting their natural shape. **3.** Apply white matte shadow to the upper immovable lid to lift up the eyebrow line visually. Accentuate the inner eye corner with the same shadow. **4.** Draw a line with brown matte shadow a little above the eyelid crease so that it will go from the outer eye corner to the base of the eyebrow. Smudge the line thoroughly to make it look like a shadow. **5.** Contour the lower lid from the inside with a black pencil. Contour the upper eyelid accentuating the outer eye corner. **6.** Color the eyelashes thoroughly with black lengthening mascara. **7.** Use a pencil close to the lip co or as a foundation for lip makeup. **8.** Apply a light beige moisturizing lip color to the lips. **9.** To finish, apply beige blusher correcting the facial contours.

FRANÇAIS

1. Unifiez le teint du visage en appliquant un fond de teint matifiant de ton proche de celui de la carnation de la peau. **2.** Soulignez le contour naturel des sourcils avec un crayon gris-brun en corrigeant leur forme. **3.** Soulevez la ligne des sourcils visuellement en éclaircissant les arcades sourcilières avec des fards à paupières blancs mats. Utilisez ces ombres également pour faire ressortir également le coin interne de l'œil. **4.** Dessinez une ligne un peu au-dessus du pli palpébral avec des ombres à paupières brunes mates en remontant sur l'arcade du coin externe de l'œil vers la base du sourcil. Repassez bien la ligne pour qu'elle devienne une ombre. **5.** Tracez un contour près des cils de la paupière inférieure, à l'intérieur de l'œil, avec un crayon noir. Faites un trait sur la paupière supérieure en accentuant le coin externe de l'œil. **6.** Appliquez soigneusement un mascara noir effet volume. **7.** Utilisez un crayon à lèvres de ton naturel qui servira de base pour un rouge à lèvres. **8.** Mettez un rouge à lèvres hydratant beige clair. **9.** Pour terminer le maquillage, balayez à l'aide de fards à joues beiges en corrigeant l'ovale du visage.

DEUTSCH

1. Ein mattierender Concealer, der eine Nuance heller ist, als Ihr Hautton, verleiht Ihnen einen ebenmäßigen Teint. **2.** Betonen Sie die Augenbrauen mit einem hellen, beigefarbenen Lidschatten, der die natürliche Form korrigiert. **3.** Tragen Sie einen weißen, matten Lidschatten auf das bewegliche Oberlid auf, um die Augenbrauen optisch anzuheben. Betonen Sie den inneren Augenwinkel mit dem gleichen Lidschatten. **4.** Ziehen Sie direkt über der Oberlidfalte mit braunem, mattem Lidschatten eine Linie vom äußeren Augenwinkel zur Augenbraue. Verwischen Sie diese Linie gründlich, um einen Schatteneffekt zu erhalten. **5.** Ziehen Sie das untere Augenlid von innen mit einem schwarzen Stift nach. Ziehen Sie die Konturen des Oberlids nach, um den äußeren Augenwinkel zu betonen. **6.** Tragen Sie schwarze, wimpernverlängernde Mascara auf. **7.** Verwenden Sie einen Lipliner in ihrer natürlichen Lippenfarbe als eine Foundation für die Lippenfarbe. **8.** Tragen Sie einen hellen, beigefarbenen Lippenstift auf. **9.** Vervollständigen Sie den Look mit einem beigefarbenen Rouge zur Korrektur der Gesichtskonturen.

ESPAÑOL

1. Emparejar el cutis con base mate de un tono semejante al de la piel. **2.** Acentuar las cejas con sombra beige claro corrigiendo su forma natural. **3.** Aplicar sombra mate blanca al párpado superior inmóvil para levantar visualmente la línea de la ceja. **4.** Trazar una línea con una sombra mate de color marrón un poco por encima del pliegue del párpado para que vaya desde el borde externo del ojo hasta la base de la ceja. Esfumar la línea completamente para que semeje una sombra. **5.** Contornear el párpado inferior desde la parte interna con lápiz negro. Contornear el párpado superior acentuando el borde externo. **6.** Pintar completamente las pestañas con máscara alargadora negra. **7.** Usar un lápiz de un color semejante al tono de los labios como base para maquillar la boca. **8.** Aplicar labial humectante de color beige claro en los labios. **9.** Para finalizar, aplicar rubor beige corrigiendo el contorno facial.

1

2

3

4

5

6

7

8

9

Model: Alyona Alyoshina

FROM LIGHT TO SHADOW

ENGLISH
1. Mask problem skin areas with a natural color concealer a tone lighter than the natural skin color. **2.** Even the skin tone using a make-up foundation which matches the tone of your skin. **3.** Apply a loose powder with a matte finish to the face to add velvetiness to the skin. **4.** With a light shadow, line the eyes from inner corner to outer corner. **5.** Emphasize the eye volume with grey and brown shadow coloring the lower lid and the upper lid fold, accentuating the round eye shape. **6.** Use black matte shade to accentuate the outer eye corner. Extend the color outward on the upper lid with black eyeliner lengthening the eye visually. **7.** Apply black eyeliner to the inner side- this will make the glance more expressive. Apply volume mascara to the eyelashes. **8.** Apply beige color glossy lip shine, and subtle peach-like rouge to refresh the face to the cheekbones.

FRANÇAIS
1. Dissimulez les imperfections du visage avec un correcteur de teint de couleur naturelle avec un ton plus clair que celui de la carnation de la peau. **2.** Unifiez le teint du visage avec un fond de teint de couleur proche de celle de la carnation. **3.** Balayez le visage d'un nuage d'une poudre de teint libre, pour rendre la peau plus veloutée. **4.** Dessinez un trait net sur la paupière mobile supérieure et dans le coin interne de l'œil avec des ombres blanches en poudre libre. **5.** Intensifiez le regard par application d'ombres à paupières neutres gris-brun sur la paupière inférieure et dans le creux palpébral en mettant l'accent sur l'arrondi de l'œil. **6.** Utilisez des ombres à paupières mates noires pour avoir le coin externe de l'œil de couleur plus soutenu. Faites un trait prononcé avec un eye-liner sur la paupière supérieure pour allonger visuellement l'œil. **7.** Dessinez un contour de l'œil près des cils, à l'intérieur de l'œil, ce qui rendra le regard plus expressif. **8.** Mettez un mascara avec un effet volume sur les cils. Sur les lèvres, appliquez un gloss laqué de ton beige. Adoucissez les pommettes avec un blush couleur pêche, ce qui apportera de l'éclat au visage.

DEUTSCH
1. Kaschieren Sie Problemzonen mit einem natürlichen Concealer, der eine Nuance heller ist als Ihr Teint. **2.** Verwenden Sie eine Make-up Foundation in Ihrem Hautton, um einen ebenmäßigen Teint zu erhalten. **3.** Tragen Sie einen leichten, matten Puder auf, um Ihrer Haut Samtigkeit zu verleihen. **4.** Betonen Sie die Augen vom inneren zum äußeren Augenwinkel mit einem hellen Lidschatten. **5.** Betonen Sie die Augen mit einem grauen und braunen Lidschatten. Tragen Sie diese auf das untere Augenlid und die obere Augenlidfalte auf, um den Augen eine runde Form zu verleihen. **6.** Verwenden Sie schwarzen, matten Lidschatten, um den äußeren Augenwinkel zu betonen. Verlängern Sie das Auge optisch, indem Sie die Farbe mit schwarzem Eyeliner über den äußeren Augenwinkel hinaus verlängern. **7.** Tragen Sie schwarzen Eyeliner im inneren Augenrand auf, um den Augen mehr Ausdruck zu verleihen. Tragen Sie Volumen-Mascara auf. **8.** Tragen Sie beigefarbenen Lipgloss und ein dezentes pfirsichfarbenes Rouge auf die Wangenknochen auf, um einen frischen Look zu erhalten.

ESPAÑOL
1. Ocultar las áreas problemáticas de la piel con corrector de color natural en un tono más claro que el de la piel. **2.** emparejar el tono de la piel usando una base de maquillaje que combine con el tono de la piel.
3. Aplicar polvo volátil con acabado mate en el rostro para darle un aspecto aterciopelado. **4.** Con una sombra clara, delinear los ojos desde el borde interno al borde externo. **5.** enfatizar el volumen del ojo con una sombra gris y marrón pintando el párpado inferior y el pliegue del párpado superior, pronunciando la forma redonda del ojo. **6.** Usar un tono negro mate para acentuar el borde externo del ojo. Extender el color hacia fuera sobre el párpado superior con delineador negro, alargando visualmente el ojo. **7.** Aplicar delineador negro al lado interno- esto dará más expresividad a la mirada. Aplicar máscara para el volumen en las pestañas. **8.** Aplicar brillo labial de color beige, y un rojo tipo durazno sutil en los pómulos para refrescar la cara.

1

2

3

4

5

6

7

8

Model: Maria Schevyova

CHARMED

ENGLISH 1. Start with a concealer one tone lighter than your skin to hide any imperfections. **2.** To even your complexion, apply a self-tanning foundation, avoiding the T-zone and the under eye areas. **3.** Apply light-reflecting powder to smooth the areas between the concealer and foundation and to make the skin shine. **4.** Apply light golden creamy eye-shadow to the inner corner of the eye, the upper eyelid, all the way to the brow. Darken the upper eyelid with deep golden shadow. **5.** Apply dark brown eye-shadows with golden highlights to the outer corner of the eye and the upper eyelid crease. Blend them carefully. Then fill in eyebrows with light brown matte shadow. **6.** To refresh the complexion, apply light bronze blusher to the cheekbones. **7.** Then pencil the eye from the inner side with a black eye liner. Apply lengthening mascara to the eyelashes. **8.** As a finishing touch, apply a semilucent pink gloss to lips. Voila!

FRANÇAIS

1. Dissimulez les imperfections du visage avec un correcteur de teint de couleur naturelle avec un ton plus clair que celui de la carnation de la peau. **2.** Pour unifier le teint du visage, appliquez un fond de teint effet bronzant sur la peau en évitant la zone « T » et la région sous les yeux. **3.** Appliquez une poudre aux pigments réflecteurs de lumière sur le visage, pour fondre la limite entre le correcteur et le fond de teint et pour apporter à la peau une douce luminosité. **4.** Etalez des ombres à paupières claires dorées en crème dans le coin interne de l'œil, sur la paupière mobile et sur l'arcade sourcilière. Rehaussez l'arcade sourcilière avec un ton saturé doré. **5.** Appliquez des ombres brun foncé au brillant d'or dans le coin externe de l'œil et dans le creux palpébral. Estompez-les bien pour fondre les ombres. Ensuite accentuez la ligne des sourcils avec des ombres brun clair.
6. Pour rafraîchir le teint du visage, balayez les pommettes avec un blush en poudre couleur bronze à l'aide d'une houppette. **7.** Faites le contour de l'œil, à l'intérieur de la paupière, avec un crayon noir. Couvrez bien les cils avec un mascara allongeant.
8. A la fin du maquillage, appliquez un gloss de couleur semi-transparente donnant un effet scintillant.

DEUTSCH

1.Beginnen Sie mit einem Concealer, der eine Nuance heller ist als Ihr Hautton, um Problemzonen zu kaschieren. **2.** Tragen Sie eine selbstbräunende Foundation auf, um einen ebenmäßigen Teint zu erhalten. Vermeiden Sie hierbei die T-Zone und den Bereich unter den Augen. **3.** Tragen Sielichtreflektierenden Puder auf, um Concealer und Foundation zu verbinden und der Haut einen gewissen Glanz zu verleihen. **4.** Tragen Sie hellgoldenen Creme-Lidschatten im inneren Augenwinkel, oberen Augenlid und bis zur Augenbraue auf. Tragen Sie auf das obere Augenlid einen dunkleren, vollen Goldton auf.
5. Tragen Sie im äußeren Augenwinkel und auf die obere Lidfalte einen dunkelbraunen Lidschatten mit goldenen Highlights auf. Verwischen Sie diese leicht. Betonen Sie Ihre Augenbrauen mit einem hellbraunen, matten Lidschatten. **6.** Tragen Sie ein helles, bronzefarbenes Rouge auf Ihre Wangenknochen auf, um einen frischen Teint zu erhalten. **7.** Tragen Sie nun schwarzen Eyeliner und wimpernverlängernde Mascara auf.
8. Vervollständigen Sie Ihren Look mit einem halb-transparenten pinkfarbenen Lipgloss. Voila!

ESPAÑOL

1. Comenzar con un corrector un tono menor que el de la piel para esconder cualquier imperfección.
2. Para emparejar el cutis, aplicar una base autobronceante evitando la zona de la T y el área bajo los ojos.
3. Aplicar polvo luminoso para suavizar las áreas entre el corrector y la base y para dar más brillo a la piel.
4. Aplicar sombra cremosa de color dorado claro en el borde interior del ojo, el párpado superior, hasta la ceja. Oscurecer el párpado superior con sombra dorado profundo.
5. Aplicar sombra marrón oscuro con reflejos dorados al borde externo de los ojos y al pliegue del párpado superior. Fundirlas entre sí cuidadosamente. Luego, rellenar la zona de la ceja con sombra mate de color marrón claro. **6.** Para dar frescura al cutis, aplicar rubor de color bronce claro en los pómulos. **7.** Delinear el ojo desde el lado interno con lápiz negro. Aplicar máscara para alargar de color negro sobre las pestañas.
8. Como toque final aplicar un labial semibrillante de color rosa a los labios y ¡Voilà!

Model: Anastasiya Pavlova

COFFEE WITH CINNAMON

ENGLISH

1. To make the makeup look natural, apply crisp powder of two shades: the lighter one – to the - zone, under the eyes and to the chin, the darker one – to the lateral parts of the forehead, the cheekbones and to the alae of the nose. **2.** Highlight the natural eyebrow line with light taupe shadow, style the hair of the eyebrows in the required direction with transparent gel accentuating the sharp ends. **3.** Apply white matte shadow to the upper eyelid. Highlight the inner eye corner with the same shadow. **4.** Accentuate the upper eyelid crease with beige shadow, smudge the borders thoroughly. **5.** Contour the lower eyelid from the inside with a black pencil, contour the eye following the lash line accentuating the outer eye corner. Draw a bright arrow from the lower eyelid. **6.** Smudge the pencil line on the lower eyelid with dark brown shadow. **7.** Color the eyelashes with lengthening mascara. **8.** Apply a light beige matte lip color to the lips. **9.** To make the makeup tender, apply peach-like powder instead of blusher to the cheekbones.

FRANÇAIS

1. Pour obtenir pour un éclat naturel, passez une poudre libre de deux teintes : appliquez celle qui est la plus claire sur la « T-zone », sous les yeux et sur le menton ; mettez celle qui est plus foncée sur les tempes, les pommettes et sur les ailes des narines. **2.** Soulignez la ligne naturelle des sourcils avec des ombres à paupières gris-brun, arrangez-les en appliquant un gel capillaire incolore, pour les diriger dans le sens souhaité. Portez bien attention aux pointes fourchues. **3.** Etalez des ombres à paupières blanches sur la paupière supérieure. Eclaircissez également le coin interne de l'œil. **4.** Accentuez le pli palpébral supérieur avec des ombres à paupières beiges, fondez bien les limites. **5.** Dessinez un trait à l'intérieur de la paupière inférieure avec un crayon noir. Faites un contour de l'œil au ras des cils en mettant l'accent sur le coin externe de l'œil. Dessinez un « trait d'eye-liner » soutenu qui part du coin externe de la paupière inférieure. **6.** Estompez le « trait d'eye-liner » sur la paupière inférieure avec des ombres brun foncé. **7.** Mettez un mascara allongeant sur les cils. **8.** Mettez un rouge à lèvres opaque de ton beige clair. **9.** Pour adoucir le maquillage, balayez les pommettes avec un halo de poudre pêche.

DEUTSCH

1. Ein frischer Puder in zwei Farbtönen verleiht Ihnen einen natürlichen Look. Tragen Sie den helleren Puderton auf die T-Zone, unterhalb der Augen und auf das Kinn auf. Tragen Sie den dunkleren Farbton auf die seitlichen Stirnpartien, die Wangenknochen und den Nasenrücken auf. **2.** Betonen Sie die natürliche Form der Augenbrauen mit einem graubraunen Lidschatten. Bringen Sie die Augenbrauen mit einem transparenten Gel in Form und betonen Sie die spitz zulaufenden Enden. **3.** Tragen Sie weißen matten Lidschatten auf das untere Augenlid und den inneren Augenwinkel auf. **4.** Betonen Sie die obere Augenlidfalte mit beigefarbenem Lidschatten. Verwischen Sie die Ränder gründlich. **5.** Ziehen Sie die Konturen des unteren Augenlids von innen mit einem schwarzen Stift nach. Wiederholen Sie dies entlang des Wimpernrands zur Betonung des äußeren Augenwinkels. Zeichnen Sie einen hellen Pfeil vom unteren Augenlid weg. **6.** Verwischen Sie die Linie am Unterlid mit einem dunkelbraunen Lidschatten. **7.** Betonen Sie die Wimpern mit einerwimpernverlängernden Mascara. **8.** Tragen Sie einen hellen, beigefarbenen Lippenstift auf. **9.** Tragen Sie anstelle von Rouge einen pfirsichfarbenen Puder auf die Wangenknochen auf, um einen dezenten Look zu erhalten.

ESPAÑOL

1. Para que el maquillaje luzca natural, aplicar sombra radiante de dos tonos: el más claro- para la zona de la T, para el área bajo los ojos y para la pera; el más oscuro para la zona lateral de la frente, par las mejillas y para las alas de la nariz. **2.** Destacar la línea natural de la ceja con una sombra marrón topo, modelar el cabello de la ceja hacia la dirección requerida con gel transparente acentuando el extremo en punta. **3.** Aplicar sombra mate color blanco al párpado superior. Resaltar el borde interno del ojo con la misma sombra. **4.** Acentuar el pliegue del párpado superior con una sombra beige, esfumar los bordes completamente. **5.** Contornear el párpado inferior desde el interior con un lápiz negro, contornear el ojo siguiendo la línea de las pestañas acentuando el borde del ojo. Trazar una flecha línea definida desde el párpado inferior. **6.** Esfumar la línea del lápiz sobre el párpado inferior con una sombra de color marrón oscuro. **7.** Pintar las pestañas con una máscara alargadora **8.** Aplicar un labial mate de color beige claro en los labios. **9.** Para suavizar el maquillaje aplicar un polvo tipo durazno, en vez de aplicar rubor en los pómulos.

1

2

3

4

5

6

7

8

9

Model: Maria Buchanenko

COLOR IS THE SOUL OF ANY MAKE-UP. BRIGHT, SOMETIMES EVEN FANCY SHADES BRING ABOUT SPECIAL MOOD. THIS SECTION INTRODUCES YOU TO THE MOST DIFFERENT TYPES OF COLOR HARMONY, YOU WILL LEARN COLORS COMBINATION TECHNIQUES AND... DISCOVER AN ARTISTIC TALENT IN YOURSELF!

LA COULEUR, C'EST L'ÂME DE TOUT MAQUILLAGE. QU'ELLES SOIENT VIVES, OU PARFOIS MÊME AVEC DES NUANCES FANTAISISTES, LES COULEURS NOUS METTENT DANS DES HUMEURS PARTICULIÈRES. DANS CETTE SECTION VOUS ALLEZ DÉCOUVRIR LES ALLIANCES HARMONIQUES DE COULEURS LES PLUS VARIÉES, VOUS APPROPRIER LES TECHNIQUES DE COMBINAISONS DE TONS... ET VOUS DÉCOUVRIR DES TALENTS D'ARTISTE !

FARBE IST DIE SEELE DES MAKE-UPS. HELLE, MANCHMAL AUSGEFALLENE FARBEN ERWECKEN EINE BESONDERE STIMMUNG. IN DIESEM ABSCHNITT FINDEN SIE DIE UNTERSCHIEDLICHSTEN FARBKOMBINATIONEN UND FARBTECHNIKEN. ENTDECKEN SIE DEN KÜNSTLER IN IHNEN!

EL COLOR ES EL ALMA DE TODO MAQUILLAJE. TONOS BRILLANTES E INCLUSO, A VECES, EXTRAVAGANTES, GENERAN SIEMPRE UN ESTADO DE ÁNIMO ESPECIAL. ESTA SECCIÓN TE PRESENTA LOS MÁS VARIADOS TIPOS DE ARMONÍAS DE COLORES, APRENDERÁS TÉCNICAS PARA LA COMBINACIÓN DE COLORES Y...
¡DESCUBRIRÁS TU TALENTO ARTÍSTICO!

BIRD OF PARADISE

ENGLISH

1. To even the skin relief and make the face shine, use light reflecting foundation close to the skin tone. **2.** Accentuate the eyebrows with a taupe pencil correcting their natural shape. **3.** Apply light violet pearl creamy shadow to the upper eyelid. **4.** Color the lower lid with bright blue shadow accentuating the outer eye corner. Highlight the inner eye corner with white peal shadow. **5.** Contour the whole eye with a dark blue pencil, draw a clear V-shape on the upper immovable lid to lift up the outer eye corner. **6.** Color the inner corner of the upper lid with bright pink shadow accentuating the eyelid crease. **7.** Smudge the pencil with dark blue shadow laying a color emphasis on the outer eye corner to attach it an almond-like shape. **8.** Complete the color palette with pearl shadow with a green tint, applying it under the eyebrow and slightly smudging the adjacent colors. **9.** Color the eyelashes with lengthening mascara thoroughly. **10.** Apply bright pink matte shadow to the cheekbones. Apply delicate pink shimmery gloss to the lips.

FRANÇAIS

1. Pour lisser la peau et apporter de la luminosité au visage, utilisez un fond de teint contenant des pigments réflecteurs de lumière de couleur proche de celle de la carnation. **2.** Marquez le contour des sourcils en corrigeant leur forme naturelle avec un crayon gris-beige. **3.** Appliquez des ombres à paupières nacrées de texture crème et de couleur mauve clair sur la paupière supérieure. **4.** Passez une ombre bleu vif sur la paupière inférieure en accentuant le coin externe de l'œil. Eclaircissez le coin interne de l'œil avec du nacre blanc. **5.** Faites le contour de l'œil entier avec un crayon bleu foncé. Soulevez visuellement l'angle externe de l'œil en dessinant un angle bien visible en forme de « V » sur la paupière immobile du haut. **6.** Déposez une ombre rose vif dans le coin interne de la paupière supérieure en accentuant les plis palpébraux. **7.** Estompez le trait du crayon avec une ombre bleu foncé, en rendant le coin externe plus soutenu et en lui apportant une forme d'amande. **8.** Pour enrichir la palette chromatique, ajoutez une ombre nacrée aux reflets verts sur l'arcade sourcilière et estompez légèrement les couleurs voisines. **9.** Maquillez les cils soigneusement avec un mascara allongeant. **10.** Appliquez un blush mat couleur rose vif sur les pommettes. Sur les lèvres, appliquez un gloss scintillant légèrement rose.

DEUTSCH

1. Verwenden Sie einen lichtreflektierenden Concealer, der eine Nuance heller ist, als Ihr Hautton, um einen ebenmäßigen und strahlenden Teint zu erhalten. **2.** Betonen Sie die Augenbrauen mit einem graubraunen Stift zur Korrektur der natürlichen Form. **3.** Tragen Sie einen hellvioletten cremigen Lidschatten mit Perlmuttglanz auf das Oberlid auf. **4.** Verwenden Sie einen hellblauen Lidschatten für das untere Augenlid und betonen Sie den äußeren Augenwinkel. Betonen Sie den inneren Augenwinkel mit einem weißen Lidschatten mit Perlmuttschimmer. **5.** Ziehen Sie die Konturen des gesamten Auges mit einem dunkelblauen Stift nach und gestalten Sie eine deutliche V-Form auf dem unbeweglichen oberen Augenlid, um den äußeren Augenwinkel anzuheben. **6.** Tragen Sie einen hellrosa Lidschatten in den inneren Augenwinkel des Oberlids auf und betonen Sie die Augenlidfalte. **7.** Verwischen Sie die Linie mit einem dunkelblauen Lidschatten und bringen Sie das Auge durch Betonung des äußeren Augenwinkels in eine Mandelform. **8.** Vervollständigen Sie die Farbkombination mit einem leicht grünlichen Lidschatten mit Perlmuttschimmer unterhalb der Augenbraue und verwischen Sie diesen leicht mit den angrenzenden Farben. **9.** Tragen Sie ausreichend wimpernverlängernde Mascara auf. **10.** Tragen Sie einen hellrosa Lidschatten auf die Wangenknochen und ein zartes, rosa-schimmerndes Lipgloss auf.

ESPAÑOL

1. Para emparejar la piel, descongestionarla y darle brillo, utilizar una base luminosa de un tono semejante a la piel. **2.** Acentuar las cejas con un lápiz marrón topo corrigiendo su natural. **3.** Aplicar sombra cremosa perlada de color violeta claro en el párpado superior. **4.** Pintar el párpado inferior con sombra azul brillante acentuando el borde externo del ojo. Resaltar el borde interno del ojo con una sombra blanca perlada. **5.** Contornear todo el ojo con lápiz azul oscuro. Trazar una forma de V en el párpado superior fijo para levantar el borde externo del ojo. **6.** Pintar el borde interno del párpado superior con una sombra de color rosa brillante. **7.** Esfumar el lápiz con sombra azul oscura enfatizando el color de borde externo del ojo para darle la forma de una almendra. **8.** completar la paleta de colores con una sombra perlada de tintes verdes, aplicándola bajo la ceja y esfumándola, apenas, sobre el color adyacente. **9.** Pintar completamente las pestañas con máscara alargadora. **10.** Aplicar sombra mate de color rosa brillante a los pómulos. Aplicar un labial rosa delicado con destellos sobre los labios.

1

2

3

4

5

6

7

8

9

10

Model: Ekaterina Ukhanova

SUN FESTIVAL

ENGLISH

1. Mask problem skin areas with a concealer a tone lighter than the natural skin color. Even the complexion with a natural tone mattifying concealer. **2.** Accentuate the natural eyebrow line with a taupe pencil, style the eyebrows with transparent gel in the proper direction. **3.** Color the upper and lower eyelids with pearl shadow of a red tone accentuating the outer eye corner. **4.** Accentuate the outer eye corner with brick-red shadow. **5.** Apply bright red blusher to the cheekbones, and also to the temples connecting it with the shadow. **6.** Color the eyelashes with black mascara. **7.** Apply red and golden gloss to the lips.

FRANÇAIS

1. Camouflez les imperfections du visage avec un correcteur de teint d'un ton plus clair que celui de la carnation de la peau. Pour unifier le teint du visage, utilisez un fond de teint matifiant de couleur naturelle. **2.** Soulignez la ligne naturelle des sourcils avec un crayon gris-brun, arrangez-les en appliquant un gel capillaire incolore, pour les discipliner. **3.** Passez une ombre à paupières de ton roux nacré sur les paupières supérieures et inférieures en accentuant le coin externe de l'œil. **4.** Renforcez le coin externe de l'œil par application d'ombres de couleur brique. **5.** Etalez un blush de couleur brique vif sur les pommettes, mettez-les également sur le haut des parties latérales du front en les ramenant vers les ombres sur les paupières. **6.** Mettez un mascara noir sur les cils. **7.** Appliquez un gloss de nuance roux-doré sur les lèvres.

DEUTSCH

1. Tragen Sie einen Concealer, der eine Nuance heller ist, als Ihr Hautton auf, um Problemzonen zu kaschieren. Ein natürlicher, mattierender Concealer verleiht Ihnen einen ebenmäßigen Ton. **2.** Betonen Sie die natürliche Form der Augenbraue mit einem graubraunen Stift. Bringen Sie die Augenbrauen mit einem transparenten Gel in Form. **3.** Tragen Sie einen rötlichen Lidschatten mit Perlmuttschimmer auf das Ober- und Unterlid auf und betonen Sie dabei den äußeren Augenwinkel. **4.** Betonen Sie den äußeren Augenwinkel mit einem ziegelroten Lidschatten. **5.** Tragen Sie hellrotes Rouge auf die Wangenknochen und Schläfen auf und verbinden Sie dieses mit dem Lidschatten. **6.** Tragen Sie schwarze Mascara auf. **7.** Vervollständigen Sie den Look mit rotem und goldenem Lipgloss.

ESPAÑOL

1. Ocultar las áreas problemáticas de la piel con un corrector de un tono menor que el de la piel. Emparejar el cutis con un corrector mate de color natural. **2.** Acentuar la línea natural de la ceja con un lápiz de color marrón topo, modelar las cejas con un gel transparente en la dirección correcta. **3.** Pintar los párpados superiores e inferiores con una sombra perlada de un tono rojizo acentuando el borde externo del ojo. **4.** Acentuar el borde exterior del ojo con una sombra rojo ladrillo. **5.** Aplicar un rubor de color rojo brillante en los pómulos y en la zona de las sienes, conectándola con la sombra. **6.** Pintar las pestañas con una máscara negra. **7.** Aplicar un labial rojo y dorado en los labios.

Model: Irina Artyshko

ELEMENT OF FIRE

ENGLISH

1. Even the skin tone with light reflecting foundation. **2.** Style the hair of the eyebrows with transparent gel in the proper direction. **3.** Color the upper eyelid with red and orange matte shadow rounding out the eye shape and accentuating the outer eye corner. **4.** Accentuate the lower lid with bright yellow shadow, smudge the orange shadow with it laying an emphasis on the outer eye corner. **5.** Draw a clear arrow line with a liquid eyeliner on the upper eyelid. Apply black lengthening mascara to the eyelashes. **6.** To refresh the skin tone apply delicate pink blusher with a glowing effect. **7.** To finish the makeup, apply pale beige lip color.

FRANÇAIS

1. Pour unifier le teint du visage, utilisez un fond de teint aux pigments réflecteurs de lumière. **2.** Gainez les sourcils avec un gel capillaire incolore, pour les arranger dans le sens souhaité. **3.** Etendez des ombres rouge-orange mates sur la paupière supérieure en arrondissant la forme de l'œil et en accentuant le coin externe de l'œil. **4.** Dessinez une ligne sur la paupière inférieure avec des ombres jaune vif, fondez-les avec des ombres oranges en mettant accent sur le coin externe. **5.** Faites un trait d'eye-liner liquide sur la paupière supérieure. Mettez un mascara noir volumateur sur les cils. **6.** Rehaussez l'éclat du visage en appliquant un blush rose pâle effet illuminé. **7.** A la fin, mettez un rouge à lèvres de couleur beige pâle.

DEUTSCH

1. Ein lichtreflektierender Puder verleiht Ihnen einen ebenmäßigen Teint. **2.** Bringen Sie die Augenbrauen mit einem transparenten Gel in Form. **3.** Tragen Sie roten und orangefarbenen, matten Lidschatten auf das Oberlid auf, um die runde Form der Augen und den äußeren Augenwinkel zu betonen. **4.** Betonen Sie das untere Augenlid mit einem hellgelben Lidschatten. **5.** Ziehen Sie eine pfeilartige Linie mit flüssigem Eyeliner entlang des Oberlids. Tragen Sie schwarze, wimpernverlängernde Mascara auf. **6.** Tragen Sie einen zarten rosa Rougeton auf, um der Haut einen frischen und strahlenden Look zu verleihen. **7.** Vervollständigen Sie das Make-up mit einem hellen, beigefarbenen Lippenstift.

ESPAÑOL

1. Emparejar el tono de la piel con una base luminosa. **2.** Modelar el pelo de las cejas con un gel transparente en la dirección correcta. **3.** Pintar el párpado superior con una sombra mate de color rojo anaranjado rellenando la forma del ojo para acentuar el borde externo del ojo. **4.** Acentuar el párpado inferior con una sombra de color amarillo brillante, esfumarla con la sombra anaranjada para enfatizar el borde externo del ojo. **5.** Trazar una línea clara con un delineador líquido sobre el párpado superior. Aplicar una máscara alargadora de color negro en las pestañas. **6.** Para realzar el tono de la piel, aplicar un rubor de color rosa delicado con efecto luminoso. **7.** Para finalizar el maquillaje, aplicar un labial beige pálido en los labios.

1

2

3

4

5

6

7

Model: Margarita Kochkina @ Fashion

ROSE GARDEN

ENGLISH

1. Even the skin tone with light reflecting foundation. **2.** Accentuate the natural eyebrow line with a taupe pencil, style the eyebrows with transparent gel in the proper direction. **3.** Color the upper eyelid with pink shadow accentuating to outer eye corner. **4.** Correct the eye contour with shades of two colors. Apply pale pink, almost white shadow to the inner eye corner and under the eyebrow, accentuating the outer eye corner with dark pink shadow. **5.** Draw a thin arrow line with a grey pearl eyeliner on the upper eyelid to lift the outer eye corner visually. **6.** Color the eyelashes with black lengthening mascara. **7.** Refresh the skin tone with delicate pink blusher. **8.** To finish the makeup with pale pink lip gloss.

FRANÇAIS

1. Pour unifier le teint du visage, utilisez un fond de teint aux pigments réflecteurs de lumière. **2.** Soulignez la ligne naturelle des sourcils avec un crayon contour des yeux gris-brun, arrangez-les dans le sens souhaité en appliquant un gel capillaire incolore. **3.** Passez une ombre rose sur la paupière supérieure en accentuant le coin externe de l'œil. **4.** Corrigez la forme de l'œil avec des ombres de deux couleurs. Appliquez des ombres rose pâle, qui tendent vers blanc, à l'intérieur de la paupière et sur l'arcade sourcilière, et des ombres rose foncé à l'extérieur de la paupière. **5.** Marquez un trait d'œil de biche avec un eye-liner gris nacré sur la paupière supérieure en remontant visuellement le coin externe de l'œil. **6.** Mettez un mascara noir allongeant sur les cils. **7.** Rehaussez l'éclat du visage en appliquant un blush rose pâle. **8.** Terminez le maquillage en appliquant un brillant de ton rose pâle sur les lèvres.

DEUTSCH

1. Ein lichtreflektierender Concealer verleiht Ihnen einen ebenmäßigen Ton. **2.** Betonen Sie die natürliche Form der Augenbrauen mit einem graubraunen Stift. Bringen Sie die Augenbrauen mit einem transparenten Gel in Form. **3.** Tragen Sie einen rosa Lidschatten auf das untere Augenlid auf und betonen Sie den äußeren Augenwinkel. **4.** Korrigieren Sie die Augenkontur mit zwei Farben. Tragen Sie einen hellrosa, nahezu weißen Lidschatten auf den inneren Augewinkel und unterhalb der Augenbraue auf. Betonen Sie den äußeren Augenwinkel mit einem dunkelrosa Lidschatten. **5.** Ziehen Sie eine dünne pfeilartige Linie mit einem grauen Eyeliner mit Perlmuttschimmer auf dem oberen Augenlid, um den äußeren Augenwinkel optisch anzuheben. **6.** Tragen Sie schwarze, wimpernverlängernde Mascara auf. **7.** Ein zartes rosa Rouge verleiht Ihrer Haut die nötige Frische. **8.** Vervollständigen Sie den Look mit einem hellrosa Lipgloss.

ESPAÑOL

1. Emparejar el tono de la piel con una base luminosa. **2.** Acentuar la línea natural de la ceja con un lápiz marrón topo, modelar las cejas con un gel transparente en la dirección correcta. **3.** Pintar el párpado superior con sombra rosa acentuando el borde externo del ojo. **4.** Corregir el contorno de los ojos con sombras de dos colores. Aplicar rosa pálido, casi blanco en el borde interno del ojo y debajo de las cejas. Para acentuar el borde externo del ojo utilizar una sombra rosa más oscura. **5.** Trazar una línea con delineador de color gris nacarado sobre el párpado superior para levantar visualmente el borde externo del ojo. **6.** pintar las pestañas con una máscara alargadora negra. **7.** realzar el tono de la piel con un rubor rosa delicado. **8.** Finalizar el maquillaje con un labial rosa pálido.

1

2

3

4

5

6

7

8

Model: Maria Buchanenko

NAME OF THE ROSE

ENGLISH

1. Apply mattifying foundation to the face. **2.** Style the eyebrows with transparent gel in the proper direction. **3.** Apply pale pink shadow to the upper and lower eyelids. **4.** Color the upper movable lid with a bright pink pencil finishing it with an arrow at the outer eye corner. **5.** Accentuate the outer eye corner with black matte shadow to make the pink arrow clearer. **6.** Color the eyelashes with black mascara. **7.** Apply light matte blucher of pink color to the cheekbones and cheeks. **8.** Apply a pale pink pencil to the lips leaving them matte.

FRANÇAIS

1. Appliquez un fond de teint matifiant. **2.** Gainez les sourcils à l'aide d'un gel capillaire incolore en les arrangeant dans le sens souhaité. **3.** Etalez une ombre rose pâle sur les paupières supérieures et inférieures. **4.** Posez un crayon contour des yeux rose vif sur la paupière mobile supérieure en dessinant un trait avec un petit crochet sur le coin externe de l'œil. **5.** Soulignez le coin externe de l'œil avec des ombres noir mat, pour rehausser le trait rose. **6.** Mettez un mascara noir sur les cils. **7.** Balayez les pommettes et les joues avec un blush léger rose mat. **8.** Pour terminer le maquillage remplissez les lèvres avec un crayon à lèvres rose pâle en les laissant mates.

DEUTSCH

1. Tragen Sie einen mattierenden Concealer auf. **2.** Bringen Sie die Augenbrauen mit einem transparenten Gel in Form. **3.** Tragen Sie einen hellen, pinkfarbenen Lidschatten auf Ober- und Unterlid auf. **4.** Tragen Sie mit einem hellen, pinkfarbenen Stift Farbe auf das bewegliche Unterlid auf und vervollständigen Sie diesen Schritt mit einem Pfeil im äußeren Augenwinkel. **5.** Betonen Sie den äußeren Augenwinkel mit schwarzem, mattem Lidschatten, um den rosa Pfeil hervorzuheben. **6.** Tragen Sie schwarze Mascara auf. **7.** Betonen Sie die Wangenknochen und Wangen mit einem leicht mattierten, rosafarbenen Rouge. **8.** Vervollständigen Sie den Look mit einem blassrosa Lipliner mit mattiertem Effekt.

ESPAÑOL

1. Aplicar base matizadora en el rostro. **2.** Modelar las cejas con un gel transparente en la dirección correcta. **3.** Aplicar una sombra rosa pálido en el párpado superior y en el inferior. **4.** Pintar el párpado móvil superior con un lápiz de color rosa brillante, finalizar con una línea en el borde externo del ojo. **5.** Acentuar el borde externo del ojo con una sombra mate de color negro para destacar la línea rosa. **6.** pintar las pestañas con una máscara negra. **7.** Aplicar un rubor mate de color rosa en los pómulos y en las mejillas. **8.** Aplicar un lápiz rosa pálido en los labios, dejarlos en tono mate.

1

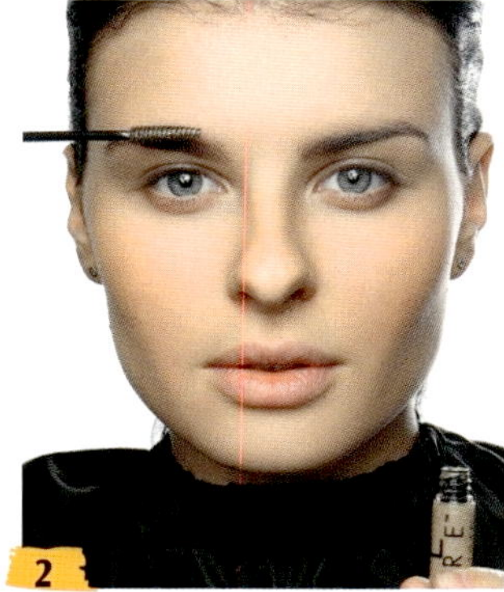
2

3

4

5

6

7

8

Model: Elizaveta Kashirina

SUNFLOWER

ENGLISH
1. Even out skin tone with a powder foundation close to the natural skin tone. **2.** For definition, apply a neutral bronze powder under cheekbones, along the sides of the nose and around the temples and hairline.
3. Define brows with taupe shadow, and style with clear brow gel.
4. Sweep a maroon shadow into the upper eyelid crease, slightly rounding the corner for a wide-eyed effect.
5. Pat a sunny yellow powder shadow across upper lid. **6.** Accentuate the lower lid with a golden powder shadow, patting a bit extra into the inner eye-corner. Blend the area where the maroon and yellow shadows meet to avoid a harsh edge. **7.** Line lower lashes with a black pencil, and line upper lids with slight "wing" at outer corner. **8.** Coat lashes with black mascara. **9.** Apply a glossy nude tone lip gloss warmed with gold.

FRANÇAIS
1. Pour unifier le teint du visage et lui apporter de la luminosité, utilisez un fond de teint à fines particules réflectrices de lumière de couleur proche de celle de la carnation de la peau.
2. Balayez une poudre à effet bronzant sur les pommettes, les ailes des narines, puis en suivant le contour du front, pour donner plus d'arrondi au visage. **3.** Soulignez la ligne naturelle des sourcils avec une ombre gris-brun, arrangez-les en appliquant un gel capillaire incolore. **4.** Appliquez une ombre couleur bordeaux dans le pli palpébral supérieur en arrondissant la paupière et en accentuant le coin externe de l'œil. **5.** Passez une ombre jaune vif sur la paupière mobile supérieure. **6.** Soulignez la paupière inférieure avec une ombre en poudre libre dorée en accentuant le coin interne de l'œil. Fondez la limite en l'estompant entre les ombres bordeaux et jaune. **7.** Marquez le contour au ras des cils à l'intérieur de la paupière inférieure avec un crayon contour des yeux noir. Dessinez un trait au ras des cils de la paupière supérieure, du plus fin au plus épais vers le coin externe de l'œil. **8.** Mettez un mascara noir allongeant sur les cils. **9.** Appliquez un brillant de ton doré sur les lèvres.

DEUTSCH
1. Tragen Sie eine Puder-Foundation, die Ihrem Teint entspricht, auf, um einen ebenmäßigen Teint zu erhalten.
2. Tragen Sie ein neutrales bronzefarbenes Puder unterhalb der Wangenknochen, entlang der Nasenseiten, der Schläfen und entlang dem Haaransatz auf, um Kontur zu erhalten.
3. Betonen Sie Ihre Augenbrauen mit einem graubraunen Lidschatten und bringen Sie diese mit einem Augenbrauengel in Form. **4.** Tragen Sie mit einem kleinen Pinsel einen kastanienbraunen Lidschatten auf die obere Lidfalte auf. Runden Sie die Ecken ab, um die Augen größer erscheinen zu lassen. **5.** Tragen Sie ein sonniges gelbes Puder auf den Oberlidbereich auf. **6.** Betonen Sie das untere Augenlid mit dem gleichen Lidschatten und tragen Sie etwas mehr im inneren Augenwinkel auf. Verwischen Sie den Bereich mit einem kastanienbraunen und gelben Lidschatten, um harte Kanten zu vermeiden. **7.** Tragen Sie auf den unteren Augenrand schwarzen Eyeliner auf und lassen Sie die Linie am oberen Augenrand über den Augenwinkel hinauslaufen.
8. Betonen Sie Ihre Wimpern mit schwarzem Mascara. **9.** Vervollständigen Sie den Look mit einem Nude-Lipgloss mit warmen Goldtönen.

ESPAÑOL
1. Emparejar el tono de la piel con una base en polvo de un tono semejante al de la piel. **2.** Por definición, aplicar un polvo de color bronce neutro debajo de los pómulos, al costado de la nariz y alrededor de la frente y la línea del pelo. **3.** Definir las cejas con una sombra de color marrón topo y modelarlas con un gel para cejas.
4. Esparcir sombra granate en el pliegue del párpado superior, bordeando apenas el extremo para lograr un efecto de ojos grandes. **5.** Dar pequeños toques con sombra de color amarillo soleado en los párpados.
6. Acentuar el párpado inferior con sombra en polvo de color de oro, con algunos toquecitos extras en el borde interno del ojo. Fundir el área del encuentro entre la sombra amarilla y la granate, evitar un borde áspero.
7. Delinear bajo los ojos con lápiz negro, y delinear los párpados con una pequeña saliente en el borde externo. **8.** Dar una capa de máscara negra sobre las pestañas. **9.** Aplicar un labial color piel y dorado.

1

2

3

4

5

6

7

8

9

Model: Anna Smirnova

SUMMER COLOR

ENGLISH

1. Use a light-textured, matt foundation in two different shades to accentuate bone structure. Use the lighter one to shade the T-zone, under eye and chin area; the darker one on either sides of the forehead, wings of nose, cheekbones, and cheeks. Blend thoroughly. **2.** Underline the eyebrows with grey-brown shadows. Highlight the inner eye corner at both upper and lower lash line with white pencil and pearl shadows and thoroughly blend.
3. Apply a small amount of transparent gel to shape and set eyebrows, emphasizing their natural form.
4. Highlight the outer eye corner with dark green pencil, accentuating and extending the line of the upper and lower lashes and the line of the eyelid upwards and outwards. **5.** Apply shadows of rich green shades with pearl effect on foundation created with the dark pencil. **6.** Extend limits of dark shadows above the crease using golden pearlescent shades of the lightest green, extended up into brow area to highlight. **7.** Use black mascara with volumizing effect. Apply beige-pink blusher with light-reflecting particles on cheek-bones to highlight bone structure. **8.** Match the contour of lips with a nude pencil as close to natural shade as possible. Apply nude gloss for sultry effect.

FRANÇAIS

1. Appliquez un fond de teint matifiant en combinant les deux teints : un teint plus clair sur la T-zone, la zone sous les yeux et le menton, et un autre plus foncé sur les tempes, les ailes des narines, les pommettes et les joues.
2. Soulignez les sourcils avec une ombre gris-brun. Eclaircissez le coin interne de l'œil et sous les sourcils avec un crayon contour blanc, ensuite estompez bien les traits. **3.** Sculptez les sourcils à l'aide d'un gel incolore en gardant leur contour naturel. Utilisez un crayon contour vert foncé pour accentuer le coin externe de l'œil, pour dessiner un contour des cils inférieurs et supérieurs, et pour souligner la limite de la paupière mobile supérieure. **4.** Appliquez une ombre à paupières de couleur anis vif aux accents nacrés sur la base créée avec le crayon contour blanc. **5.** Passez une ombre vert vif à effet scintillant pardessus le contour vert foncé. **6.** Fondez les limites des ombres avec une ombre nacrée et dorée. Marquez le contour de la paupière inférieure, sur la muqueuse de l'œil, avec le crayon vert foncé. **7.** Mettez un mascara noir voluminateur sur les cils. Dessinez le contour des lèvres avec un crayon à lèvres de ton proche de celui de la carnation. Balayez les pommettes avec un fard à joues rose-beige à fines particules réflectrices de lumière. **8.** Remplissez les lèvres avec un brillant à lèvres scintillant de tonalité naturelle.

DEUTSCH

1. Verwenden Sie eine leichte, matte Foundation in zwei Nuancen, um die Gesichtsform zu betonen. Verwenden Sie den helleren Ton für die T-Zone, unterhalb der Augen und im Kinnbereich. Verwenden Sie den dunkleren Ton seitlich der Stirn, auf den Nasenflügeln, Wangenknochen und Wangen. Verblenden Sie die zwei Nuancen gründlich. **2.** Betonen Sie den Bereich unterhalb der Augenbrauen mit grün-braunem Lidschatten. Betonen Sie den inneren Augenwinkel, sowohl am oberen, als auch am unteren Wimpernrand mit einem weißen Kajal und perlmuttfarbigen Lidschatten. Verwischen Sie das ganze.
3. Tragen Sie etwas Augenbrauengel auf, um diese in Form zu bringen und deren natürliche Form zu betonen.
4. Betonen Sie den äußeren Augenwinkel mit einem dunkelgrünen Kajal und betonen und verlängern Sie den oberen und unteren Wimpernrand nach oben und außen. **5.** Tragen Sie satte Grüntöne mit Perlmutteffekt auf,die mit dem dunkleren Stift geschaffene Foundation auf.
6. Erweitern Sie die dunklen Lidschatten oberhalb der Lidfalte bis hin zu den Augenbrauen mit goldenen Perlmutttönen in einem Hellgrün.
7. Tragen Sie einen Volumen-Mascara und ein beige-pinkes Rouge mit lichtreflektierenden Partikeln auf die Wangenknochen auf, um die Wangenknochen zu betonen. **8.** Betonen Sie die Kontur Ihrer Lippen mit einemLipliner in Nude-Farben, der dem natürlichen Farbton Ihrer Lippen ähnlich ist. Vervollständigen Sie den Look mit einem Lipgloss in Nude-Tönen.

ESPAÑOL

1. Aplicar un corrector mate combinando dos tonos: acentuar la zona de la T, las áreas debajo de los ojos, y la pera; los laterales de la frente, las alas de la nariz, párpados y mejillas, con uno más oscuro. **2.** Acentuar las cejas con una sombra de color marrón topo. Marcar el borde interno de los ojos y el párpado inferior con un lápiz blanco, esfumarlo completamente. **3.** Modelar las cejas con un gel translúcido para acentuar su forma natural. Destacar el borde externo del ojo con un lápiz verde oscuro, para dar énfasis a las líneas interior y superior de las pestañas y a la línea del párpado móvil. **4.** Aplicar una sombra intensa de color verde claro con efecto nacarado sobre la base hecha por el lápiz blanco.
5. Aplicar una sombra intensa de color verde con efecto brillante sobre el lápiz verde oscuro. **6.** Esfumar los bordes de la sombra con una sombra perlada color dorado. Contornear el ojo desde adentro con un delineador verde oscuro. **7.** Pintar las pestañas con una máscara para alargar de color negro. Contornear los labios con un lápiz de color semejante al labio. Aplicar un rubor luminoso de color beige y rosa en los pómulos.
8. Aplicar brillo de un tono natural en los labios.

1

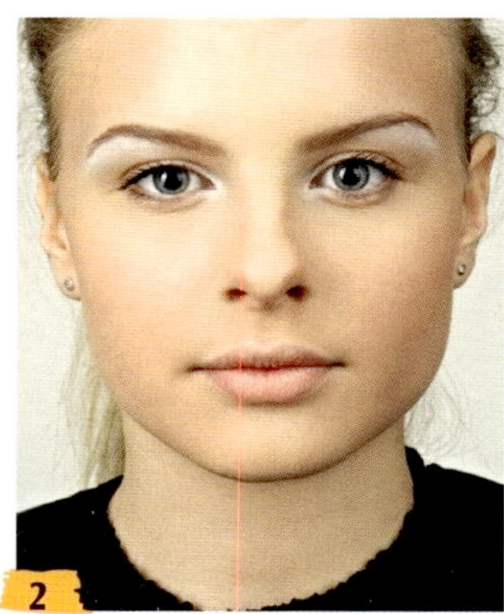
2

3

4

5

6

7

8

Model: Elizaveta Kashirina

PURPLE DIVA

ENGLISH

1. Even the skin tone with light reflecting foundation. **2.** To make the face look natural, use semitransparent powder. Style the eyebrows with transparent gel in the proper direction. **3.** Color the upper movable lid and outer eye corner with a white eyeliner. **4.** Apply white pearl shadow above the eyeliner. **5.** Accentuate the upper eyelid crease and the outer corner of the lower lid with pink and violet matte shadow. Smudge the shadow to round out the eye visually. **7.** Smudge the pencil line with black matte shadow accentuating the outer eye corner. Highlight the corner of the upper eyelid crease. **8.** Color the eyelashes with black lengthening mascara. Apply several layers to get a "spider leg" effect. **9.** To refresh the complexion, apply delicate pink creamy blusher with a glowing effect. **10.** To finish the makeup, apply pale pink lip gloss.

FRANÇAIS

1. Unifiez le teint du visage, en utilisant un fond de teint à fines particules réflectrices de lumière. **2.** Pour apporter au visage un éclat naturel, prenez une poudre translucide. Sculptez les sourcils à l'aide d'un gel incolore et dirigez-les dans le sens souhaité. **3.** Eclaircissez le coin interne de l'œil et la paupière supérieure avec un crayon contour blanc. **4.** Appliquez une ombre blanc nacré au-dessus des lignes créées par le crayon blanc. **5.** Accentuez le creux de la paupière et le coin externe de la paupière inférieure avec une ombre rose-mauve opaque. Estompez les ombres pour arrondir visuellement la forme de l'œil. **6.** Faites un contour bien visible de l'œil avec un crayon contour noir. **7.** Estompez le contour noir avec une ombre noir mat, en accentuant le coin externe de l'œil. Soulignez l'angle du pli palpébral. **8.** Maquillez les cils avec un mascara noir effet volume. Passez le mascara plusieurs fois pour donner un effet de faux cils. **9.** Rehaussez l'éclat du visage en mettant un fard à joues rose pâle capteur de lumière pour un effet illuminé. **10.** A la fin, appliquez un gloss rose pâle sur les lèvres.

DEUTSCH

1. Eine lichtreflektierende Foundation verleiht Ihnen einen ebenmäßigen Teint. **2.** Verwenden Sie einen halbtransparenten Puder für einen natürlichen Look. Bringen Sie die Augenbrauen mit einem transparenten Gel in Form. **3.** Tragen Sie mit einem weißen Eyeliner Farbe auf das bewegliche Oberlid und den äußeren Augenwinkel auf. **4.** Tragen Sie weißen Lidschatten mit Perlmuttschimmer oberhalb des Eyeliners auf. **5.** Betonen Sie die Oberlidfalte und den äußeren Augenwinkel des Unterlids mit einem matten, violetten und rosa Lidschatten. Verwischen Sie die Ränder gründlich. **7.** Verwischen Sie die Linie des Eyeliners mit schwarzem Lidschatten und betonen Sie den äußeren Augenwinkel. Betonen Sie die Ecke der oberen Augenlidfalte. **8.** Tragen Sie schwarze, wimpernverlängernde Mascara auf. Tragen Sie mehrere Schichten auf, um den sogenannten „Spinnenbein"-Effekt zu erhalten. **9.** Tragen Sie ein dezentes, rosafarbenes cremiges Rouge auf, um einen frischen, strahlenden Teint zu erhalten. **10.** Vervollständigen Sie den Look mit hellrosa Lipgloss.

ESPAÑOL

1. Emparejar el tono de la piel con una base luminosa. **2.** Para una apariencia natural, usar polvo semitransparente. Modelar las cejas co un gel transparente en el sentido adecuado. **3.** Pintar el párpado superior móvil y el borde externo del ojo con un delineador blanco. **4.** aplicar una sombra perlada de color blanco sobre el delineador. **5.** Acentuar el pliegue del párpado superior y el extremo externo del ojo del párpado inferior con sombra mate rosa y violeta. Esfumar la sombra para completar visualmente el ojo. **7.** Esfumar la línea del lápiz con sombra mate negra, destacando el borde externo del ojo. Resaltar el borde del pliegue del párpado superior. **8.** Pintar las pestañas con máscara negra para alargar. Aplicar varias capas para lograr un efecto "pestaña postiza". **9.** Para realzar el cutis, aplicar un rubor cremoso rosa delicado con efecto luminoso. **10.** Para finalizar el maquillaje, aplicar un labial rosa pálido.

1

2

3

4

5

6

7

8

9

10

Model: Valeriya Popova

HUMMINGBIRD

ENGLISH

1. To even the complexion, apply a matte foundation close to the skin tone. **2.** Correct the face shape with neutral blusher. **3.** Apply bright violet shadow to the upper movable lid. **4.** Accentuate the upper lid fold, and also the outer and inner corners of the movable lid with bright blue shadow. **5.** Blend the blue color with light green shadow to lengthen the eye visually. **6.** Apply light beige shadow to the lower lid. **7.** Apply lengthening mascara to the eyelashes. Contour the lower lid from inside and the upper lid from outside. Accentuate the natural shape of eyebrows with a beige pencil. **8.** As a finishing touch, apply a rose-pink gloss to the lips.

FRANÇAIS

1. Pour unifier le teint du visage, appliquez un fond de teint matifiant de couleur proche de celle de la carnation de la peau. **2.** Apportez des corrections au visage adaptées à sa morphologie en appliquant un fard à joues de couleur neutre. **3.** Appliquez une ombre à paupières mauve vif sur la paupière mobile supérieure. **4.** Renforcez le pli palpébral de la paupière supérieure avec une ombre bleu vif, ainsi que les coins interne et externe de l'œil. **5.** Fondez bien l'ombre bleue à l'aide d'une ombre vert clair pour allonger la forme des yeux. **6.** Etalez une ombre beige clair sur la paupière inférieure. **7.** Appliquez soigneusement un mascara effet volume. Tracez un contour à l'intérieur de la paupière inférieure et au-dessus des cils de la paupière supérieure avec un crayon contour noir. Soulignez la ligne naturelle des sourcils. **8.** Finalisez le maquillage en appliquant un brillant à lèvres rose-pâle.

DEUTSCH

1. Tragen Sie eine matte Foundation, die Ihrem Hautton entspricht auf, um einen ebenmäßigen Teint zu erhalten. **2.** Korrigieren Sie die Gesichtsform mit einem natürlichen Rougeton. **3.** Tragen Sie hellen violetten Lidschatten auf das obere bewegliche Augenlid auf. **4.** Betonen Sie die obere Lidfalte und die äußeren und inneren Winkel des beweglichen Augenlids mit einem strahlend blauen Lidschatten. **5.** Verwischen Sie den bläulichen Lidschatten mit einem hellgrünen Lidschatten, um das Auge optisch zu strecken. **6.** Tragen Sie auf das untere Augenlid hellen, beigefarbenen Lidschatten und wimpernverlängernde Mascara auf Ihre Wimpern auf. **7.** Verleihen Sie dem unteren Augenlid von innen und dem oberen Augenlid von außen Kontur.Betonen Sie die natürliche Form Ihrer Augenbrauen mit einem beigefarbenen Augenbrauenstift. **8.** Tragen Sie zur Vervollständigung des Looks noch ein rosapinkes Lipgloss auf.

ESPAÑOL

1. Para emparejar el cutis, aplicar una base mate de un color semejante al tono de la piel. **2.** Corregir la forma de la cara con un rubor de color neutral. **3.** Aplicar sombra violeta brillante al párpado superior móvil. **4.** Acentuar el doblez del párpado superior, y también los bordes internos y externos del párpado móvil con sombra azul brillante. **5.** Fundir el color azul con una sombra verde clara para alargar visualmente el ojo. **6.** Aplicar una sombra beige clara en el párpado inferior. **7.** Aplicar una máscara alargadora a las pestañas. Contornear el párpado inferior desde adentro y el párpado superior desde afuera. Acentuar la forma natural de las cejas con un lápiz beige. **8.** Como toque final, aplicar un labial rosado.

1

2

3

4

5

6

7

8

Model: Loucine Ananyan

OCEAN OF LOVE

ENGLISH

1. Even the skin tone with light reflecting foundation. Make the skin tone more natural with semitransparent powder. **2.** Accentuate the natural shape of the eyebrows with light taupe shadow. Style them with transparent gel in the proper direction.
3. Accentuate the volume of the upper eyelid with beige matte shadow. **4.** Color the lower eyelid with a white pencil.
5. Draw arrows with a black liquid eyeliner through the whole upper eyelid accentuating the outer eye corner.
6. Highlight the outer eye corner with bright blue shadow; when applied over the white pencil the shadow will look even brighter. **7.** Color the eyelashes with lengthening mascara.
8. To avoid cracking of lip color, contour the lips and color them entirely with a bright red matte pencil. **9.** Apply a rich red lip color to the lips. **10.** To refresh the skin tone apply delicate pink blusher with a glowing effect.

FRANÇAIS

1. Unifiez le teint du visage, en utilisant un fond de teint à fines particules réflectrices de lumière. Pour apporter au visage un éclat naturel, prenez une poudre translucide.
2. Soulignez la ligne naturelle des sourcils avec un crayon contour gris-brun. « Brossez » les sourcils dans le sens souhaité et fixez-les à l'aide d'un gel incolore. **3.** Renforcez la largeur de la paupière supérieure par application des ombres beige mat.
4. Dessinez une ligne le long des cils sur la paupière inférieure. **5.** Prenez un eye-liner fluide pour faire un trait le long de toute la paupière supérieure, s'affinant sur le coin externe.
6. Avec une ombre bleu vif accentuez le coin externe de la paupière inférieure. Les ombres se mettent d'autant plus en valeur que vous les appliquez au-dessus du contour blanc. **7.** Mettez un mascara effet volume sur les cils.
8. Pour éviter les bavures, marquez le contour des lèvres et remplissez les lèvres entièrement avec un crayon contour des lèvres mat de couleur rouge vif. **9.** Mettez un rouge à lèvres rouge vif. **10.** Rehaussez l'éclat du visage avec un fard à joues rose velouté aux reflets scintillants.

DEUTSCH

1. Tragen Sie eine lichtreflektierende Foundation auf, um einen ebenmäßigen Teint zu erhalten. Ein halbtransparenter Puder verleiht Ihnen einen natürlichen Teint. **2.** Betonen Sie die natürliche Form der Augenbrauen mit einem hellen graubraunen Lidschatten. Bringen Sie diese mit einem transparenten Gel in Form. **3.** Betonen Sie das obere Augenlid mit einem matten, beigefarbenen Lidschatten. **4.** Tragen Sie einen weißen Kajal auf das untere Augenlid auf.
5. Zeichnen Sie mit einem schwarzen Flüssig-Eyeliner Pfeile über das gesamte obere Augenlid, um den äußeren Augenwinkel zu betonen.
6. Betonen Sie den äußeren Augenwinkel mit einem hellen blauen Lidschatten. Durch den zuvor aufgetragenen weißen Stift, wirkt der Lidschatten noch heller. **7.** Tragen Sie wimpernverlängernde Mascara auf.
8. Ziehen Sie die Lippenkonturen mit einem matten roten Stift nach und malen diese komplett aus, um eine ebenmäßige Lippenfarbe zu erhalten.
9. Tragen Sie einen knallroten Lippenstift auf. **10.** Verwenden Sie ein zart-rosafarbenes Rouge mit einem strahlenden Effekt.

ESPAÑOL

1. Emparejar el tono de la piel con una base luminosa. Hacer el tono de la piel más natural con polvo semitransparente. **2.** Acentuar la forma natural de la ceja con una sombra marrón topo. Modelarlas con gel transparente en la dirección adecuada. **3.** Acentuar el volumen del párpado superior con sombra beige mate.
4. Pintar el párpado inferior con un lápiz blanco. **5.** Trazar una línea con delineador líquido negro. A lo largo del párpado superior acentuando el borde externo del ojo. **6.** Resaltar el borde externo del ojo con una sombra azul brillante, al aplicarse sobre la línea se vuelve más brillante.
7. Pintar las pestañas con una máscara negra alargadora. **8.** Para evitar que los labios se agrieten, contornearlos completamente con un labial mate de color rojo brillante. **9.** Aplicar un labial rojo intenso a los labios.
10. Para realzar el tono de la piel, aplicar un rubor de color rosa delicado con efecto brillante.

Model: Maria Buchanenko

ULTRAMARINE

ENGLISH

1. Even the complexion with mattifying foundation close to the skin tone. **2.** To create a base for shadow, color the upper and lower eyelids with an aquamarine soft color smudging the borders thoroughly. **3.** Apply bright blue shadow to the upper eyelid crease and outer corner of the lower eyelid. Accentuate the inner corner of the lower eyelid and the center of the upper movable lid with bright green shadow to give an effect of voluminous color. **4.** Smudge the color shadow borders with white pearl shadow. **5.** Accentuate the natural eyebrow line with a taupe pencil, style the eyebrows with transparent gel in the proper direction. **6.** Outline the lower eyelid with a black pencil, contour the eye along the lash line smudging the pencil line and accentuating the outer eye corner.
7. Refresh the skin tone with delicate peach-like blusher. **8.** To finish the makeup, apply pale peach-like lip gloss.

FRANÇAIS

1. Pour unifier le teint du visage, appliquez un fond de teint matifiant couleur de la peau. **2.** Appliquez sur les paupières supérieures et inférieures un crayon gras de nuance aigue-marine, qui servira de base pour l'application des ombres. Fondez bien les limites des traits. **3.** Etalez une ombre à paupières de couleur bleu foncé vif dans le pli palpébral et le coin externe de la paupière inférieure. Ensuite avec une ombre vert vif accentuez le coin interne de la paupière inférieure et au milieu de la paupière mobile supérieure, ces couleurs donneront ainsi du relief.
4. Estompez les limites des ombres irisées avec une ombre blanche nacrée. **5.** Soulignez la ligne naturelle des sourcils avec un crayon contour gris-brun. « Brossez » les sourcils dans le sens souhaité et fixez-les à l'aide d'un gel incolore. **6.** Dessinez une ligne le long des cils sur la paupière inférieure, et au ras des cils autour de l'œil entier avec un crayon contour noir, en mettant l'accent sur le coin externe de l'œil. Estompez les traits du crayon. Prenez un mascara noir à effet allongeant. **7.** Rehaussez l'éclat du visage avec un fard à joues nuance pêche velouté. **8.** Pour finalisez le maquillage, appliquez un brillant à lèvres nuance pêche pâle sur les lèvres.

DEUTSCH

1. Tragen Sie eine mattierende Foundation auf, um einen ebenmäßigen Teint zu erhalten. **2.** Tragen Sie ein weiches Aquamarin auf das obere und untere Augenlid auf, um eine Basis für den Lidschatten zu schaffen. Verwischen Sie die Ränder gründlich. **3.** Tragen Sie einen strahlend blauen Lidschatten auf die untere Lidfalte und den äußeren Augenwinkel des unteren Augenlids auf. Betonen Sie den inneren Augenwinkel und die Mitte des oberen beweglichen Lids mit einem hellgrünen Lidschatten, um Volumen zu schaffen. **4.** Verwischen Sie die Farbränder mit einem weißen Lidschatten mit Perlmuttglanz.
5. Betonen Sie die natürliche Augenbrauenform mit einem graubraunen Stift. Bringen Sie die Augenbrauen mit einem transparenten Gel in Form.
6. Ziehen Sie die Kontur des unteren Augenlids und den Wimperrand mit einem schwarzen Stift nach und betonen Sie den äußeren Augenwinkel.
7. Ein zartes pfirsichfarbenes Rouge verleiht Ihnen einen frischen Teint.
8. Vervollständigen Sie den Look mit einem pfirsichfarbenen Lipgloss.

ESPAÑOL

1. Emparejar el cutis con una base matizadora de un tono semejante al de la piel. **2.** Para crear una base para la sombra, pintar el párpado superior y el inferior con color aguamarina suave esfumando los bordes completamente. **3.** Aplicar una sombra azul brillante al pliegue del párpado superior y al borde externo del párpado inferior. Acentuar el borde interno del párpado inferior y el centro del párpado superior móvil con sombra verde brillante para crear un efecto de color intenso. **4.** Esfumar los bordes de color de las sombras con una sombra blanca perlada.
5. Acentuar la línea natural de la ceja con un lápiz de color marrón topo, modelar la ceja con un gel transparente en la dirección adecuada.
6.Resaltar el párpado inferior con lápiz negro, contornear el ojo a lo largo de la línea de las pestañas esfumando la línea del lápiz y acentuando el borde externo del ojo.
7. Realzar el tono de la piel con un rubor tipo durazno delicado. **8.** Para finalizar el maquillaje, aplicar un labial estilo durazno pálido.

1

2

3

4

5

6

7

8

Model: Ekaterina Shevchenko

CARTE BLANCHE

ENGLISH

1. Even the skin tone with mattifying foundation. **2.** To make the face look more natural apply slightly glowing semitransparent powder. **3.** Color the lower and upper eyelids with light golden shadow. **4.** Draw a clear arrow line with a white pencil on the upper eyelid. **5.** Style the eyebrows with translucent gel accentuating their natural shape. **6.** Color the eyelashes with black lengthening mascara. **7.** To contour the lips, use two pencils: a bright pink one for the center, and a violet one for the lip corners. **8.** Apply bright pink lip color over the pencil. **9.** To finish, apply slightly shimmering pink blusher.

FRANÇAIS

1. Unifiez le teint du visage, en utilisant un fond de teint à fines particules réflectrices de lumière. **2.** Pour apporter au visage un éclat naturel, prenez une poudre translucide effet visage ; le teint est ainsi subtilement éclairé d'un halo de lumière. **3.** Passez une ombre clair doré sur les paupières supérieures et inférieures. **4.** Dessinez un trait net d'un eye-liner sur la paupière supérieure avec un crayon contour blanc. **5.** Gainez les sourcils avec un gel incolore pour les discipliner en préservant leur forme naturelle. **6.** Utilisez un mascara noir effet volumateur pour les cils. **7.** Pour tracer le contour des lèvres, utilisez deux crayons à lèvres : un rose vif pour les lignes du milieu et un mauve pour les commissures des lèvres. **8.** Recouvrez le crayon d'un rouge à lèvres rose vif. **9.** Terminez le maquillage en appliquant un fard à joues roses aux subtils reflets scintillants.

DEUTSCH

1. Eine mattierende Foundation verleiht Ihnen einen ebenmäßigen Teint. **2.** Tragen Sie einen semitransparenten Puder auf, um einen natürlichen Look zu erhalten. **3.** Tragen Sie auf das obere und untere Augenlid einen hellen, goldfarbenen Lidschatten auf. **4.** Zeichnen Sie mit einem weißen Stift eine deutliche Pfeillinie entlang des oberen Augenlids. **5.** Bringen Sie die Augenbrauen mit einem transparenten Gel in ihre natürliche Form. **6.** Tragen Sie wimpernverlängernde Mascara auf. **7.** Verwenden Sie zwei Lipliner, um die Kontur der Lippen nachzuziehen: einen hellen, rosafarbenen Lipliner für die Mitte und einen violetten für die Mundwinkel. **8.** Tragen Sie einen hellen, rosafarbenen Lippenstift auf. **9.** Vervollständigen Sie den Look mit einem leicht schimmernden Rouge.

ESPAÑOL

1. Emparejar el tono de la piel con base matizadora. **2.** Para lograr que el rostro luzca natural, aplicar polvo semitransparente apenas brilloso. **3.** Pintar el párpado superior y el inferior con una sombra de color dorado claro. **4.** Trazar una línea definida con un lápiz blanco en el párpado superior. **5.** Modelar las cejas con un gel translúcido acentuando su forma natural. **6.** Pintar las pestañas con una máscara negra para alargar. **7.** Para contornear los labios, usar dos lápices: uno rosa brillante para el centro y uno violeta para las comisuras de los labios. **8.** Aplicar color rosa brillante sobre el lápiz. **9.** Para finalizar, aplicar un rubor rosa algo destellante.

1

2

3

4

5

6

7

8

9

Model: Valeriya Popova

EVENING MAKE-UP IS A SPECIAL KIND OF ART. IT REQUIRES MORE SATURATED COLORS, BOLDER SOLUTIONS ... AND IMPECCABLE TASTE. IN THIS SECTION, WE HAVE COLLECTED EXAMPLES OF HARMONIOUS EVENING MAKE-UP WITH DETAILED DESCRIPTIONS OF ITS TECHNIQUES AND METHODS.

LE MAQUILLAGE DE SOIRÉE EST UN ART PARTICULIER. IL REQUIERT DES COULEURS PLUS RICHES, DES CHOIX PLUS AUDACIEUX… ET UN BON GOÛT AFFIRMÉ. DANS CETTE PARTIE NOUS AVONS RÉUNI DES EXEMPLES HARMONIEUX DE MAQUILLAGES DE SOIRÉE, ACCOMPAGNÉS DE LA DESCRIPTION DÉTAILLÉE DES TECHNIQUES ET MÉTHODES DE LEUR RÉALISATION.

ABEND-MAKE-UP IST EINE KUNST AN SICH. ES UMFASST GESÄTTIGTE FARBEN, MUTIGERE VARIATIONEN ... UND GUTEN GESCHMACK. IN DIESEM ABSCHNITT HABEN WIR EINIGE HARMONISCHE ABEND-MAKE-UPS MIT DETAILLIERTEN BESCHREIBUNGEN DIESER TECHNIKEN UND METHODEN ZUSAMMENGEFASST.

EL MAQUILLAJE PARA LA NOCHE ES UNA TIPO ESPECIAL DE ARTE. REQUIERE COLORES MÁS SATURADOS, SOLUCIONES MÁS AUDACES… Y UN IMPECABLE GUSTO. EN ESTA SECCIÓN, HEMOS RECOLECTADO EJEMPLOS DE MAQUILLAJES DE NOCHE ARMONIOSOS CON LA DETALLADA DESCRIPCIÓN DE SUS TÉCNICAS Y MÉTODOS.

RED FLOWER

ENGLISH

1. Even the complexion with mattifying foundation close to the skin tone. **2.** Correct the facial contours with light beige blusher accentuating the cheekbones, alae of the nose and the temples. **3.** Color the upper eyelid crease with beige golden shadow accentuating the outer eye corner. **4.** Accentuate the inner eye corner, upper movable lid and the area under the eyebrow with white pearl shadow. **5.** Correct the shape of the eyebrows with a light beige pencil, style them with translucent gel. **6.** Contour the upper lash line with a black pencil extending it with a sharp arrow line. **7.** To make the eye look more voluminous apply beige shadow with a strong pearl shine effect to the lower lid. **8.** Color the eyelashes with lengthening mascara thoroughly. **9.** To correct the lip shape, contour the lips with a red pencil from the outside. **10.** As a finishing touch, apply a red shiny gloss to the lips.

FRANÇAIS

1. Unifiez le teint du visage en appliquant un fond de teint matifiant de couleur proche de celle de la carnation de la peau. **2.** Apportez les corrections morphologiques au visage grâce aux fards à joues beige clair en mettant l'accent sur les pommettes, les ailes des narines et les tempes. **3.** Appliquez une ombre beige doré dans le pli palpébral de la paupière supérieure en accentuant le coin extérieur de l'œil. **4.** Eclaircissez le coin interne de l'œil, la paupière mobile supérieure et l'arcade sourcilière avec une ombre nacrée blanche translucide. **5.** Corrigez la forme des sourcils avec un crayon beige clair, lissez-les en mettant un gel incolore pour les sourcils. **6.** Dessinez la ligne des cils supérieurs avec un crayon contour noir, remontez le trait d'eye-liner vers le haut en l'affinant. **7.** Pour agrandir le regard, appliquez une ombre beige riche en nacre sur la paupière inférieure. **8.** Maquillez les cils avec un mascara noir allongeant. **9.** Corrigez la forme des lèvres en posant un crayon à lèvres rouge sur le périmètre des lèvres. **10.** Complétez le maquillage avec un brillant à lèvres rouge.

DEUTSCH

1. Tragen Sie eine mattierende Foundation, die ihrem Hautton entspricht auf, um einen ebenmäßigen Teint zu erhalten. **2.** Korrigieren Sie die Gesichtskonturen mit einem hellen, beigefarbenen Rouge zur Betonung der Wangenknochen, Nasenflügel und Schläfen. **3.** Tragen Sie beigefarbenen, goldenen Lidschatten auf die obere Augenlidfalte auf und betonen Sie den äußeren Augenwinkel. **4.** Betonen Sie den inneren Augenwinkel, das obere bewegliche Augenlid und den Bereich unterhalb der Augenbrauen mit einem weißen Lidschatten mit Perlmuttglanz. **5.** Korrigieren Sie die Form der Augenbrauen mit einem hellen, beigefarbenen Stift. Bringen Sie diese mit einem transparenten Gel in Form. **6.** Ziehen Sie den oberen Wimpernrand mit einem schwarzen Stift nach und verlängern Sie diese mit einer spitzen Pfeilform. **7.** Tragen Sie beigefarbenen Lidschatten mit einem starken Perlmuttglanzeffekt auf das untere Augenlid auf, um dem Auge Volumen zu verleihen. **8.** Tragen Sie wimpernverlängernde Mascara auf. **9.** Korrigieren Sie die Mundform mit einem roten Lipliner. **10.** Tragen Sie ein glänzendes,rotes Lipgloss auf, um den Look zu vervollständigen.

ESPAÑOL

1. Emparejar el cutis con base matizadora de un tono semejante al de la piel. **2.** Corregir el contorno facial con rubor beige claro, acentuando los pómulos, las alas de la nariz y las sienes. **3.** Pintar el pliegue del párpado superior con una sombra beige dorada, acentuando el borde externo del ojo. **4.** Acentuar el borde interior del ojo, el párpado superior móvil y el área debajo de las cejas con sombra perlada blanca. **5.** Corregir la forma de las cejas con un lápiz beige claro. Modelarlas con gel translúcida. **6.** Contornear la línea de las pestañas superior con un lápiz trazando una fina flecha. **7.** Para que el ojo luzca más voluminoso, aplicar sombra beige con un marcado efecto luminoso en el párpado inferior. **8.** Pintar las pestañas completamente con una máscara alargadora. **9.** Para corregir la forma de los labios, contornear los labios con un lápiz rojo por el borde externo. **10.** Como toque final, aplicar un labial rojo brillante.

Model: Viktoriya Marchenko

MUSE OF DECADENCE

ENGLISH

1. Even the complexion with mattifying foundation close to the skin tone. **2.** Correct the facial contours with ball blusher of a neutral shade. **3.** Accentuate the eyebrows with a light beige pencil correcting their natural shape. **4.** To lift the eyebrow line visually, apply white creamy shadow to the upper immovable lid. **5.** Color the upper movable and lower eyelids with a black pencil. **6.** Smudge the pencil with black matte shadow slightly sharpening the outer eye corner. **7.** Color the eyelashes with lengthening mascara thoroughly. **8.** As a foundation for the lip makeup use a maroon lipstick of a soft shade. **9.** To finish the makeup, apply bright lip color to the inner part of the lip as a bright accent.

FRANÇAIS

1. Unifiez le teint du visage en appliquant un fond de teint matifiant de couleur proche de celle de la carnation de la peau. **2.** Apportez les corrections morphologiques au visage grâce au blush compact en perles de teint naturel. **3.** Redessinez les sourcils avec un crayon beige clair en corrigeant leur forme naturelle. **4.** Pour remonter visuellement la ligne des sourcils, appliquez une ombre blanche en crème sur l'arcade sourcilière. **5.** Intensifiez le regard en appliquant un crayon noir autour des yeux, sur les lignes des paupières supérieures et inférieures. **6.** Estompez le crayon noir avec une ombre noir mat, affinez le coin externe de l'œil. **7.** Maquillez soigneusement les yeux avec un mascara noir effet volume. **8.** Utilisez un rouge à lèvres bordeaux foncé de teinte feutrée en tant que base de maquillage des lèvres. **9.** Terminez en appliquant un rouge à lèvres de couleur rouge vif vers l'intérieur des lèvres pour rehausser l'apparence des lèvres.

DEUTSCH

1. Tragen Sie eine mattierende Foundation auf, um einen ebenmäßigen Teint zu erhalten. **2.** Korrigieren Sie die Gesichtskonturen mit einem natürlichen Rouge-Ton. **3.** Betonen Sie die Augenbrauen mit einem hellen, beigefarbenen Stift, um die natürliche Form zu korrigieren. **4.** Tragen Sie einen weißen, cremigen Lidschatten auf das obere unbewegliche Augenlid auf, um die Augenbrauen optisch anzuheben. **5.** Tragen Sie mit einem schwarzen Stift Farbe auf das obere bewegliche Augenlid und das untere Augenlid auf. **6.** Verwischen Sie den Stift mit einem matten, schwarzen Lidschatten und schließen Sie diesen leicht spitz am äußeren Augenwinkel ab. **7.** Tragen Sie reichlich wimpernverlängernde Mascara auf. **8.** Verwenden Sie einen sanften, kastanienbraunen Lippenstift, um eine Foundation für das Lippen-Make-up zu erstellen. **9.** Tragen Sie einen hellen Lippenstift auf die Mundmitte auf, um einen hellen Accent zu schaffen und den Look zu vervollständigen.

ESPAÑOL

1. Emparejar el cutis con base mate de un color semejante al de la piel. **2.** Corregir el contorno facial con un rubor a bolilla de un tono neutro. **3.** Acentuar las cejas con un lápiz de color beige claro corrigiendo su natural forma. **4.** Para levantar visualmente la línea de la ceja, aplicar una sombra cremosa blanca en el párpado superior fijo. **5.** Pintar los párpados superiores fijos y los inferiores con un lápiz negro. **6.** Esfumar el lápiz con una sombra mate de color negro apenas afilando el borde externo de los ojos. **7.** Pintar las pestañas completamente con una máscara para alargar las pestañas. **8.** Como base para maquillar los labios, usar un lápiz labial granate. **9.** Para finalizar el maquillaje, aplicar un lápiz labial brillante de color a la parte interna del labio como un toque de brillo.

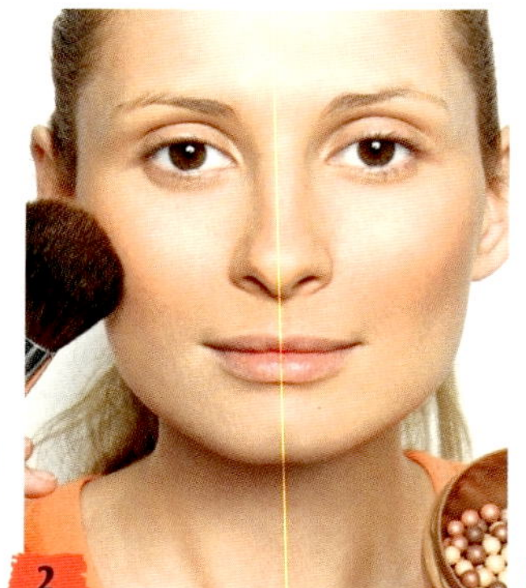

Model: Olga Cherkes

VIOLET DREAM

ENGLISH

1. Even the skin tone and mask problems of the skin with matte foundation. **2.** To make the face look more natural apply powder with a glowing effect. **3.** Style the eyebrows with golden mascara. **4.** As a foundation for shadow, apply dark violet eyeliner to the upper and lower eyelid extending the eye visually. **5.** Apply black shadow over the eyeliner smudging the borders thoroughly. **6.** Accentuate the center of the lower and upper eyelids with bright violet pearl shadow. **7.** Color the eyelashes with black lengthening mascara. **8.** Apply light beige pearl gloss to the lips. **9.** To refresh the skin tone apply pale pink blusher with a glowing effect.

FRANÇAIS

1. Unifiez le teint du visage et masquez les imperfections avec un fond de teint matifiant. **2.** Apportez un éclat naturel avec une poudre effet illuminateur. **3.** « Coiffez » les sourcils avec un mascara aux reflets dorés. **4.** Pour la base du maquillage des yeux, faites un trait mauve foncé autour des yeux en allongeant leur forme. **5.** Etalez une ombre noire sur les traits en fondant bien les limites. **6.** Accentuez le milieu des paupières inférieures et supérieures avec une ombre mauve vif nacrée. **7.** Utilisez un mascara noir effet volume. **8.** Mettez un brillant beige enrichi de nacres. **9.** Rehaussez l'éclat du visage avec des fards à joues rose pâle effet illuminateur.

DEUTSCH

1. Tragen Sie eine mattierende Foundation auf, um einen ebenmäßigen Teint zu erhalten und kleine Unregelmäßigkeiten zu kaschieren. **2.** Tragen Sie einen Puder mit Glow-Effekt auf, um einen natürlichen Look zu erhalten. **3.** Tragen Sie goldene Mascara auf die Augenbrauen auf. **4.** Tragen Sie einen dunkel-violetten Eyeliner auf das obere und untere Augenlid auf, um eine Foundation für den Lidschatten zu schaffen und das Auge optisch zu verlängern. **5.** Tragen Sie schwarzen Lidschatten über den Eyeliner auf und verwischen Sie die Ränder gründlich. **6.** Betonen Sie das obere und untere Augenlid mit einem hellen, violetten Lidschatten mit Perlmuttglanz. **7.** Tragen Sie wimpernverlängernde Mascara auf. **8.** Tragen Sie helles, beigefarbenes Lipgloss mit Perlmuttglanz auf. **9.** Tragen Sie ein blass-rosa Rouge mit Glow-Effekt auf, um einen frischen Teint zu erhalten.

ESPAÑOL

1. Emparejar el tono de la piel y ocultar sus pequeños problemas con base mate. **2.** Para lograr que la cara luzca más natural, aplicar polvo con un efecto luminoso. **3.** Modelar las cejas con máscara dorada. **4.** Como base para la sombra, aplicar delineador violeta oscuro a los párpados superiores e inferiores para agrandar visualmente el ojo. **5.** Aplicar sombra negra sobre el delineador difuminar completamente los bordes. **6.** Acentuar el centro de los párpados superior e inferior con una sombra brillante violeta perlado. **7.** Pintar las pestañas con máscara alargadora negra. **8.** Aplicar un labial beige claro perlado sobre los labios. **9.** Para realzar el tono de la piel aplicar rubor rosa pálido con un efecto luminoso.

1

2

3

4

5

6

7

8

9

Model: Anastasiya Papenkova

SMYRNA FIG

ENGLISH

1. To even the skin tone, apply crisp powder of two shades: the lighter one – to the T-zone, under the eyes and to the chin, the darker one – to the lateral parts of the forehead, the cheekbones and to the alae of the nose. **2.** Accentuate the upper eyelid under the eyebrow and inner eye corner with white creamy shadow with a radiance effect. **3.** Accentuate the upper eyelid crease with dark pink pearl shadow; smudge the shadow towards the upper immovable lid. Apply the same shadow to the lower eyelid. **4.** Accentuate the natural eyebrow line with a taupe pencil, style the eyebrows in the required direction with transparent gel laying an emphasis upon the sharp ends. **5.** Draw a neat arrow line along the upper eyelid. **6.** To make the makeup look tender apply pale pink blusher. **7.** Color the eyelashes with black lengthening mascara. **8.** Contour the lips with a maroon pencil rounding up the lips visually. **9.** To finish the makeup, apply rich maroon shiny gloss to the lips.

FRANÇAIS

1. Pour unifier le teint du visage, utilisez des poudres libres de deux teints : celle qui est la plus claire pour la zone T, sous les yeux et sur le menton, celle qui est plus foncée pour les côtés du front, les pommettes et les ailes des narines. **2.** Avec une ombre blanche en crème effet illuminateur éclaircissez la zone en-dessous des sourcils et le coin interne de l'œil. **3.** Posez une ombre rose foncé irisée dans le creux de la paupière supérieure, étendez l'ombre en l'estompant vers la paupière immobile. **4.** Soulignez la ligne naturelle des sourcils avec un crayon gris-brun, arrangez-les à l'aide d'un gel incolore pour sourcils en les dirigeant dans le sens souhaité. Portez bien attention aux extrémités pointues des sourcils. **5.** Tracez un trait de liner au plus près des cils supérieurs, remontant légèrement à la fin. **6.** Pour adoucir le maquillage, prenez un fard à joues rose pâle. **7.** Utilisez un mascara noir à effet volume. **8.** Arrondissez la forme des lèvres avec un crayon à lèvres bordeaux foncé. **9.** A la fin, mettez un brillant à lèvres de couleur bordeaux profond.

DEUTSCH

1. Tragen Sie ein frisches Puder in zwei Farbtönen auf, um einen ebenmäßigen Teint zu erhalten. Tragen Sie den helleren Ton auf die T-Zone, unterhalb der Augen und auf das Kinn auf. Verwenden Sie den dunkleren Ton für die seitlichen Stirnpartien, die Wangenknochen und Nasenflügel. **2.** Betonen Sie das obere Augenlid, unterhalb der Augenbraue und den inneren Augenwinkel mit einem weißen, cremigen Lidschatten mit Glanzeffekt. **3.** Betonen Sie die obere Augenlidfalte mit einem dunkelrosa Lidschatten mit Perlmuttglanz. Verwischen Sie diesen zum oberen Augenlid hin. Tragen Sie den gleichen Lidschatten auf das untere Augenlid auf. **4.** Betonen Sie die natürliche Augenbrauenform mit einem graubraunen Stift. Bringen Sie diese mit einem transparenten Gel in Form und betonen Sie die spitz zulaufenden Enden. **5.** Ziehen Sie eine deutliche Pfeillinie entlang des oberen Augenlids. **6.** Tragen Sie ein blass-rosa Rouge auf, um einen zarten Look zu erhalten. **7.** Tragen Sie wimpernverlängernde Mascara auf. **8.** Ziehen Sie die Lippenkonturen mit einem kastanienbraunen Lipliner nach und gestalten Sie diese optisch runder. **9.** Vervollständigen Sie das Make-up mit einem schimmernden Lipgloss in einem tiefen kastanienbraun.

ESPAÑOL

1. Para emparejar el tono de la piel, aplicar polvo radiante de dos tonos: el más claro– En la zona de la T, debajo de los ojos, y en la pera, la oscura – a los laterales de la frente, los pómulos y a las alas de la nariz. **2.** Acentuar el párpado superior debajo de la ceja y el borde interno del ojo con una sombra blanca cremosa con efecto radiante. **3.** Acentuar el pliegue del párpado superior con una sombra perlada de color rosa oscuro; difuminar hacia el párpado superior fijo. Aplicar la misma sombra sobre el párpado inferior. **4.** Acentuar la línea natural de la ceja con un lápiz de color marrón topo, modelar las cejas en la dirección adecuada con un gel transparente poniendo énfasis en las puntas afiladas. **5.** Trazar una línea de flecha nítida sobre el párpado superior. **6.** Para lograr que el maquillaje luzca más suave, aplicar rubor de color rosa pálido. **7.** Pintar las pestañas con máscara alargadora negra. **8.** Contornear los labios con un lápiz granate rellenando visualmente los labios. **9.** Para finalizar el maquillaje, aplicar un labial granate intenso a los labios.

1

2

3

4

5

6

7

8

9

Model: Evgeniya Panchenko

RUBY MAGIC

ENGLISH

1. Even the complexion with mattifying foundation close to the skin tone. **2.** Correct the facial contours and nose shape with powder of two shades. **3.** Accentuate the natural eyebrow line with taupe shadow, style the eyebrows with transparent gel in the proper direction **4.** Color the upper eyelid with henna pearl shadow; slightly accentuate the outer corner of the lower eyelid in the same way. **5.** Highlight the outer eye corner with black matte shadow accentuating the upper eyelid crease.

6. Smudge the shadow borders with white crisp shadow giving a light (-colored) accent to the area under the eyebrow; make bright the inner eye corner in the same way. **7.** Contour the eye with a black pencil from the inside; draw a bright arrow line along the upper eyelid lifting the outer eye corner visually. Color the eyelashes with black lengthening mascara.

8. Use lip gloss of a natural shade with a pearl shining effect.

FRANÇAIS

1. Unifiez le teint du visage en appliquant un fond de teint matifiant de couleur identique à celle de la carnation de la peau. **2.** Corrigez l'ovale du visage et la forme du nez avec des poudres de deux teintes. **3.** Soulignez la ligne naturelle des sourcils avec une ombre gris-brun, gainez-les à l'aide d'un gel incolore pour les discipliner. **4.** Appliquez une ombre nacrée de ton rouge brique sur la paupière supérieure, mettez une légère touche dans le coin interne de la paupière inférieure. **5.** A l'aide d'une ombre noir mat intensifiez le coin externe de l'œil en soulignant le pli palpébral. **6.** Estompez les limites des ombres avec une ombre blanche en poudre libre en apportant une touche de lumière à la zone sous les sourcils et dans le coin interne de l'œil. **7.** Dessinez la ligne d'œil sur la muqueuse avec un crayon contour des yeux noir. Tracez un trait de liner net sur la paupière supérieure, ce qui remontera visuellement l'angle externe de l'œil. Mettez un mascara noir à l'effet allongeant sur les cils.

8. Appliquez un gloss à lèvres de teinte naturelle, mais aux reflets pailletés effet mouillé.

DEUTSCH

1. Tragen Sie eine mattierende Foundation auf, um einen ebenmäßigen Teint zu erhalten. **2.** Korrigieren Sie die Gesichtskonturen und Nasenform mit einem Puder in zwei unterschiedlichen Nuancen. **3.** Betonen Sie die natürliche Augenbrauenform mit einem graubraunen Lidschatten und bringen Sie diese mit einem transparenten Geld in Form. **4.** Tragen Sie einen hennafarbenen Lidschatten mit Perlmuttglanz auf das obere Augenlid auf und betonen Sie den äußeren Augenwinkel dezent. **5.** Betonen sie den äußeren Augenwinkel und die obere Lidfalte mit einem matten, schwarzen Lidschatten. **6.** Verwischen Sie die Ränder des Lidschattens mit einem frischen, weißen Lidschatten, um dem Bereich unterhalb der Augenbraue einen hellen (farbigen) Akzent zu verpassen. Tragen Sie diesen ebenfalls auf den inneren Augenwinkel auf.

7. Ziehen Sie die Kontur des Auges mit einem schwarzen Stift von innen nach und malen Sie eine helle Pfeillinie entlang des oberen Augenlids, um den äußeren Augenwinkel optisch anzuheben. Tragen Sie wimpernverlängernde Mascara auf. **8.** Tragen Sie Lipgloss in einer natürlichen Farbe mit Perlmuttglanzeffekt auf.

ESPAÑOL

1. Emparejar el cutis con una base matizadora de un color semejante al de la piel. **2.** Corregir el contorno facial y la forma de la nariz con un polvo de dos tonos. **3.** Acentuar la línea natural de las cejas con una sombra marrón topo, modelar las cejas con un gel transparente en la dirección adecuada. **4.** Pintar el párpado superior con Sombra perlada de henna, acentuar apenas el borde externo del párpado inferior de la misma manera. **5.** Resaltar el borde externo del ojo con sombra mate negra, acentuando el pliegue del párpado superior. **6.** Difuminar los bordes de la sombra con sombra radiante de color blanca para dar un toque claro (de color) al área bajo las cejas. Que quede del mismo modo, también claro, el borde interior del ojo. **7.** Contornear el ojo con lápiz negro desde el interior; Trazar una línea sobre el párpado superior, levantando visualmente el borde externo del ojo.

8. Usar un labial de tonos naturales con un efecto nacarado resplandeciente.

Model: Irina Polyakova

CHOCOLATE-COVERED PLUM

ENGLISH

1. Even the complexion with mattifying foundation close to the skin tone. **2.** To make the makeup look more natural, use crisp powder. **3.** Accentuate the volume of the upper immovable lid and make bright the inner eye corner with white matte shadow. **4.** Color the upper eyelid crease with beige matte shadow, smudge it thoroughly. Accentuate the lower eyelid more intensively. **5.** Highlight the outer eye corner with brown matte shadow accentuating the upper eyelid crease. **6.** Accentuate the natural eyebrow shape with a beige pencil. **7.** Draw thin arrow lines along the upper eyelid with a black pencil accentuating the outer corners of the eyes. **8.** Color the eyelashes with lengthening mascara. **9.** Contour the lips with a deep brown pencil. **10.** Apply rich dark plum lip color to the lips.

FRANÇAIS

1. Pour unifier le teint du visage, appliquer un fond de teint matifiant de couleur identique à celle de la carnation de la peau. **2.** Prenez une poudre libre pour rendre le maquillage plus naturel. **3.** Faites ressortir l'arrondi de la paupière supérieure immobile à l'aide d'une ombre blanche mate. Avec la même ombre éclairez le coin interne de l'œil. **4.** Appliquez une ombre beige mate dans le creux palpébral et fondez-les bien. Etalez cette ombre avec plus d'intensité également sur la paupière inférieure. **5.** Renforcez le coin externe de l'œil avec une ombre brune mate, en mettant l'accent sur la ligne du creux palpébral. **6.** Soulignez la ligne naturelle des sourcils avec un crayon beige. **7.** Dessinez des traits fins, au ras des cils, sur la paupière supérieure en soulignant les coins externes des yeux. **8.** Mettez un mascara noir à l'effet allongeant sur les cils. **9.** Faites un contour des lèvres avec un crayon à lèvres brun foncé. **10.** Appliquez un rouge à lèvres de couleur profonde prune foncé sur les lèvres.

DEUTSCH

1. Tragen Sie eine mattierende Foundation auf, um einen ebenmäßigen Teint zu erhalten. **2.** Tragen Sie einen frischen Puder auf, um einen natürlichen Look zu erhalten. **3.** Betonen Sie das Volumen des oberen unbeweglichen Augenlids und tragen Sie einen matten, weißen Lidschatten auf den inneren Augenwinkel auf, um diesen zu betonen. **4.** Tragen Sie einen matten, beigefarbenen Lidschatten auf die obere Augenlidfalte auf und verwischen Sie diesen gründlich. Betonen Sie das untere Augenlid intensiver. **5.** Betonen Sie den äußeren Augenwinkel und somit die obere Augenlidfalte mit einem matten braunen Lidschatten. **6.** Betonen Sie die natürliche Form der Augenbraue mit einem beigefarbenen Stift. **7.** Ziehen Sie mit einem schwarzen Stift dünne Pfeillinien entlang des oberen Augenlids und betonen Sie somit den äußeren Augenwinkel. **8.** Tragen Sie wimpernverlängernde Mascara auf. **9.** Ziehen Sie die Lippenkonturen mit einem tief-braunen Stift nach. **10.** Tragen Sie eine dunkle, volle, pflaumenähnliche Farbe auf die Lippen auf.

ESPAÑOL

1. Emparejar el cutis con base matizadora de un color semejante al de la piel. **2.** Para lograr un maquillaje más natural, usar polvo radiante. **3.** Acentuar el volumen del párpado superior fijo y hacer. **4.** Pintar el pliegue del párpado superior con una sombra beige mate, difuminarla completamente. Acentuar el párpado inferior más intensamente. **5.** Resaltar el borde externo del ojo con sombra mate de color marrón acentuando el pliegue del párpado superior. **6.** Acentuar la forma natural de la ceja con lápiz beige. **7.** Trazar una línea angosta en el párpado superior con un lápiz negro acentuando el borde externo del ojo. **8.** Pintar las pestañas con máscara alargadora. **9.** Contornear con un lápiz. **10.** Aplicar un lápiz labial intenso de color ciruela oscura.

1

2

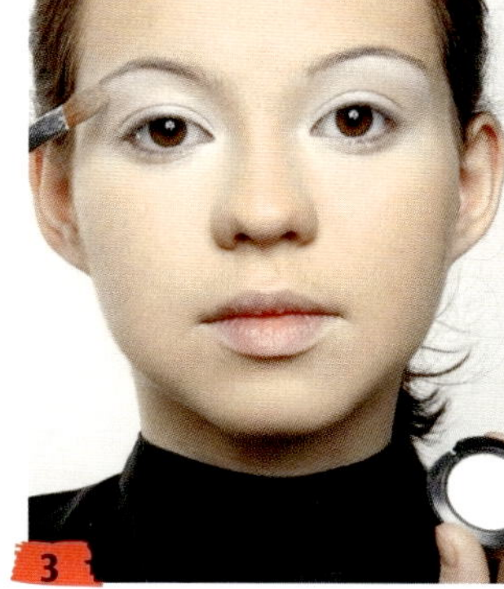
3

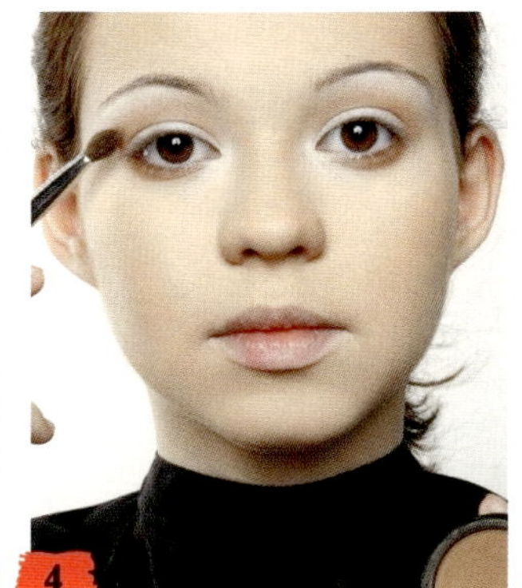
4

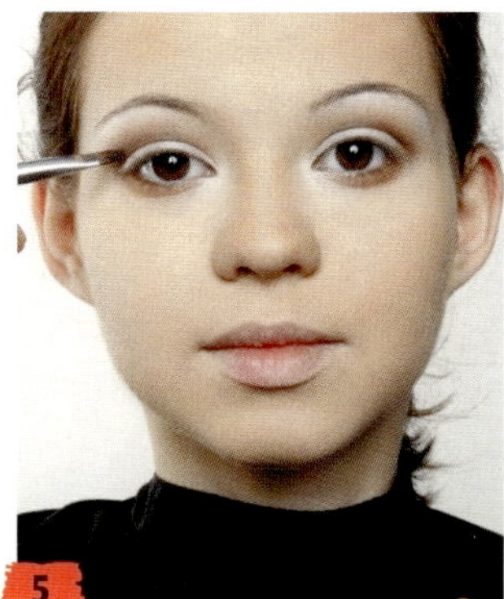
5

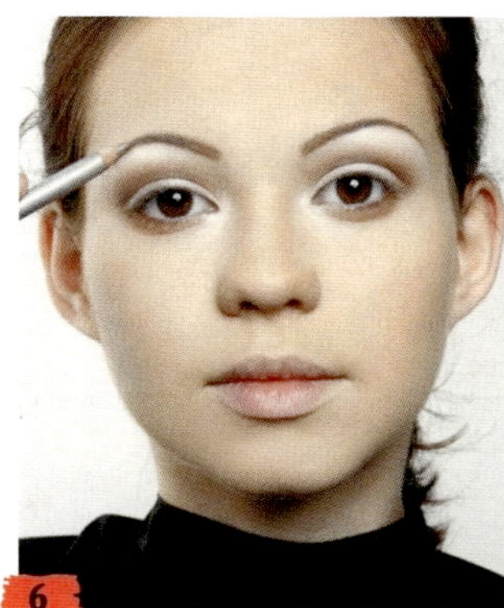
6

7

8

9

10

Model: Tatyana Valik

ATTRACTION

ENGLISH

1. Even the complexion with mattifying foundation close to the skin tone. **2.** Correct the facial contours and nose shape with powder of two shades. **3.** Accentuate the natural eyebrow line with a taupe pencil, style the eyebrows with transparent gel in the proper direction. **4.** Color the upper and lower eyelids with violet shadows. **5.** Smudge the violet color with rich pink-lilac shadow rounding up the eye shape. **6.** Smudge the borders of the color shadows with white pearl shadow. **7.** Contour the eye with a black pencil from the inside, draw a bright arrow line along the upper eyelid lifting the outer eye corner visually. **8.** Color the eyelashes with black lengthening mascara. **9.** Apply semilucent gloss of a natural pale beige shade to the lips. **10.** To refresh the skin tone apply delicate pink blusher.

FRANÇAIS

1. Pour unifier le teint du visage, appliquer un fond de teint matifiant de couleur identique à celle de la carnation de la peau. **2.** Corrigez l'ovale du visage et la forme du nez avec des poudres de deux teintes. **3.** Soulignez la ligne naturelle des sourcils avec un crayon gris-brun, fixez-les à l'aide d'un gel incolore pour les diriger dans le sens souhaité. **4.** Appliquez une ombre bleu violacé sur les paupières supérieures et inférieures. **5.** Estompez l'ombre bleu violacé avec une ombre rose violet vif en arrondissant la forme de l'œil. **6.** Estompez les limites des ombres colorées avec une ombre blanc nacré. **7.** Dessinez un contour à l'intérieur de la paupière inférieure avec un crayon contour noir. Tracez un trait de liner net le long des cils supérieurs, pour remonter le coin de l'œil visuellement vers le haut. **8.** Mettez un mascara noir allongeant sur les cils. **9.** Sur les lèvres appliquez un brillant transparent de teinte naturelle beige pâle. **10.** Rehaussez l'éclat du visage avec des fards à joues rose pâle.

DEUTSCH

1. Tragen Sie eine mattierende Foundation auf, um einen ebenmäßigen Teint zu erhalten. **2.** Korrigieren Sie die Gesichtskonturen und Nasenform mit einem Puder in zwei Nuancen. **3.** Betonen Sie die natürliche Form der Augenbrauen mit einem graubraunen Stift. Bringen Sie diese mit einem transparenten Gel in Form. **4.** Tragen Sie einen violetten Lidschatten auf das obere und untere Augenlid auf. **5.** Verwischen Sie den violetten Lidschatten mit einem Lidschatten in einem tiefen rosa-fliederfarbenen Farbton und verleihen Sie somit den Augen eine runde Form. **6.** Verwischen Sie die Ränder der Lidschattenfarben mit einem weißen Lidschatten in Perlmuttglanz. **7.** Ziehen Sie die Augenkontur mit einem schwarzen Stift von innen nach. Zeichnen Sie eine helle Pfeillinie entlang des oberen Augenlids, um den äußeren Augenwinkel optisch anzuheben. **8.** Tragen Sie eine wimpernverlängernde Mascara auf. **9.** Tragen Sie ein halb-transparentes Lipgloss in einem natürlichen Beige-Ton auf. **10.** Tragen Sie ein Rouge in einem zarten Rosa-Ton auf, um einen frischen Look zu erhalten.

ESPAÑOL

1. Emparejar el rostro con una base matizadora de un tono similar al de la piel. **2.** Corregir el contorno facial y la forma de la nariz con polvo de dos tonos. **3.** Acentuar la línea natural de la ceja con un lápiz color topo, modelar las cejas con un gel transparente en la dirección adecuada. **4.** Pintar los párpados superiores e inferiores con sombras violetas. **5.** Esfumar el color violeta con una sombra de color lila rosado intenso para completar la forma del ojo. **6.** Esfumar los bordes de las sombras de color con una sombra perlada blanca. **7.** Contornear el ojo con un lápiz negro desde el interior, trazar una flecha definida a lo largo del párpado superior elevando visualmente el borde externo. **8.** Pintar las pestañas con máscara alargadora negra. **9.** Aplicar brillo semitransparente de un tono beige pálido sobre los labios. **10.** Para realzar el tono de la piel, aplicar un rubor de un delicado tono rosa.

1

2

3

4

5

6

7

8

9

10

Model: Elena Kostina

AUTUMN ANGEL

ENGLISH

1. Even the complexion with mattifying foundation close to the skin tone. **2.** Apply golden pink light reflecting creamy blusher to the cheekbones. **3.**Accentuate the upper eyelid crease with brown shadow with light golden shine laying an emphasis upon the outer eye corner. Style the eyebrows with translucent gel accentuating their natural shape. **4.** Color the upper and lower eyelids with dark golden shadow smudging the borders. **5.** Contour the eye with a black pencil from the inside and outside making the lines thicker towards the outer eye corner, smudge the line thoroughly. **6.** To make the look more expressive color the eyelashes with lengthening mascara. **7.** Apply bright pink matte lip color to the lips, smudge the contour slightly.

FRANÇAIS

1. Pour uniformiser le relief du visage, appliquer un fond de teint matifiant d'une tonalité proche de celle de la carnation de la peau. **2.** Balayez les pommettes avec un fard à joues en crème de teinte rose doré aux fines particules réflectrices de lumière. **3.** Soulignez le pli palpébral supérieur avec une ombre brune en mettant l'accent sur le coin externe de l'œil. Dirigez les sourcils dans le sens souhaité et fixez-les à l'aide d'un gel incolore pour sourcils. **4.** Avec une ombre de teinte d'or foncé maquillez les paupières supérieures et inférieures en estompant bien les limites des ombres. **5.** Réalisez un contour à l'intérieur de la paupière inférieure et sur les cils supérieurs. Le trait se fait plus épais vers l'extérieur de l'œil. Fondez bien les traits. **6.** Pour intensifier le regard, mettez un mascara effet volume sur les cils. **7.** Appliquez un rouge à lèvres de couleur rose vif opaque et estompez légèrement le contour.

DEUTSCH

1. Tragen Sie eine mattierende Foundation in Ihrem Hautton auf, um einen ebenmäßigen Teint zu erhalten. **2.** Tragen Sie ein lichtreflektierendes, cremiges Rouge in einem Rosaton mit goldenen Effekten auf die Wangenknochen auf. **3.** Betonen Sie die obere Augenlidfalte mit einem braunen Lidschatten mit einem hellen Goldglanz und betonen Sie den äußeren Augenwinkel. Bringen Sie die Augenbrauen mit einem transparenten Geld in ihre natürliche Form. **4.** Tragen Sie einen dunklen, goldfarbenen Lidschatten auf das obere und untere Augenlid auf und verwischen Sie die Ränder. **5.** Ziehen Sie die Kontur der Augen mit einem schwarzen Stift von innen und außen nach. Lassen Sie die Linien zum äußeren Augenwinkel hin dicker werden. Verwischen Sie diese gründlich. **6.** Tragen Sie eine wimpernverlängernde Mascara auf, um den Augen mehr Ausdruck zu verleihen. **7.** Tragen Sie einen hellen, matten Lippenstift in einem Rosaton auf und verwischen Sie die Konturen leicht.

ESPAÑOL

1. Emparejar el rostro con una base matizadora de un tono similar al de la piel. **2.** Aplicar un rubor cremoso luminoso de color rosa dorado en los pómulos. **3.** Acentuar el pliegue del párpado superior con una sombra marrón con destellos dorados poniendo el énfasis en el borde externo del ojo. Modelar las cejas con un gel acentuando su forma natural. **4.** Pintar los párpados superiores e inferiores con una sombra dorada oscura y esfumar los extremos. **5.** Contornear el ojo con un lápiz negro por el interior y el exterior, haciendo que las líneas sean más anchas en el borde externo y, luego, esfumar la línea completamente. **6.** Para lograr una mirada más expresiva, pintar las pestañas con una máscara alargadora de pestañas. **7.** Aplicar un lápiz labial de color rosa mate sobre los labios, difuminar apenas el contorno.

Model: Anna Smirnova

EVEN IF YOU HAVE NEVER DREAMED OF LOOKING LIKE A SUPERSTAR, YOU WILL PROBABLY BE INTERESTED IN LEARNING TECHNOLOGIES TO CREATE "STAR" MAKE-UP. AFTER ALL, YOU CAN TEACH FROM MARILYN MONROE, AUDREY HEPBURN AND OTHER "STYLE ICONS" NOT ONLY THE ART OF DRESSING FASHIONABLY, BUT ALSO TO THE ART OF CREATING A "BILLBOARD FACE."

MÊME SI VOUS N'AVEZ JAMAIS RÊVÉ DE RESSEMBLER À UNE STAR, VOUS SEREZ SÛREMENT INTÉRESSÉE DE DÉCOUVRIR LES TECHNIQUES DE CRÉATION D'UN MAQUILLAGE DE « STAR ». APRÈS TOUT, IL EST TOUJOURS BON D'APPRENDRE AUPRÈS DE MARILYN MONROE, D'AUDREY HEPBURN OU D'AUTRES « ICÔNES » DU STYLE NON SEULEMENT L'ART D'ÊTRE BIEN HABILLÉE, MAIS ÉGALEMENT COMMENT DEVENIR « UN VISAGE EN PREMIÈRE PAGE ».

AUCH WENN SIE BISHER NICHT DAVON GETRÄUMT HABEN, WIE EIN SUPERSTAR AUSZUSEHEN, FINDEN SIE ES WAHRSCHEINLICH INTERESSANT, DIE TECHNIKEN FÜR EIN „STAR"-MAKEUP ZU LERNEN. SCHLIESSLICH KANN MAN VON MARILYN MONROE, AUDREY HEPBURN UND ANDEREN „STIL-IKONEN" NICHT NUR DIE KUNST SICH MODISCH ZU KLEIDEN LERNEN, SONDERN AUCH DIE KUNST EIN „GESICHT, WIE AUF WERBEPLAKATEN" ZU KREIEREN.

AÚN SI NUNCA HAS SOÑADO CON LUCIR COMO UNA SUPERESTRELLA, PROBABLEMENTE ESTÉS INTERESADA EN APRENDER TÉCNICAS PARA CREAR UN MAQUILLAJE "DE ESTRELLA". DESPUÉS DE TODO, PUEDES APRENDER DE MARILYN MONROE, AUDREY HEPBURN Y OTROS "ÍCONOS DEL ESTILO" NO SOLO EL ARTE DE VESTIR A LA MODA, SINO TAMBIÉN EL ARTE DE CREAR UNA "CARA DE PUBLICIDAD"

MARLENE DIETRICH STYLE

ENGLISH

1. Mask problem skin areas with a concealer of a natural light shade. Even the tone and texture of the skin with mattifying foundation. **2.** Using a white soft pencil, lift the eyebrow line visually from behind and make the upper eyelid more voluminous. Highlight the inner eye corner, sharpen the chin, straighten the nasal arch and make the cheekbone line clearer with white matte powder. Accentuate the alae of the nose with dark powder; darken the cheeks and lateral parts of the forehead. **3.** Draw the upper eyelid crease and lower eyelash line with brown shadows extending the eye and making the eyelids more voluminous. Accentuate the eye corner with dark brown shadow. Apply blusher of a natural shade to the cheekbones. **4.** Draw the eyebrows with a black pencil, and style them with translucent eyebrow gel for eyebrows. Accentuate the eye corner with a smudged arrow on the upper eyelid. Contour the lips with a maroon matte pencil. **5.** Color the upper eyelashes with mascara thoroughly setting the direction towards the outer eye corner. Use a bright red lipstick for the lips. **6.** Blot the lips with a dry tissue. Add a little blusher of a cold shade.

FRANÇAIS

1. Camouflez les imperfections de la peau et les zones à problèmes avec un correcteur de teinte naturelle claire. Unifiez le teint et le relief de la peau avec un fond de teint matifiant. **2.** Relevez la ligne des sourcils en appliquant un crayon gras blanc sur l'arcade sourcilière, arrondissez à la paupière supérieure. A l'aide d'une poudre blanche mate éclaircissez le coin interne de l'œil, rendez le menton plus pointu, redressez l'arête du nez et rendez la ligne des pommettes plus nette. Avec une poudre foncée, soulignez les ailes des narines, couvrez les joues et les côtés du front. **3.** Accentuez le pli palpébral supérieur et la ligne des cils inférieurs avec une ombre brune. Cela allongera la forme des yeux et donnera du volume aux paupières. Renforcez l'angle externe de l'œil avec une ombre brun foncé. Appliquez un fard à joues de teinte naturelle sur les pommettes. **4.** Marquez le contour des sourcils avec un crayon noir, ensuite fixez les sourcils avec un gel incolore. Accentuez le coin externe de l'œil en dessinant un trait de liner en prolongement des cils supérieurs et en estompant le trait. Faites un contour des lèvres avec un crayon à lèvres mat de couleur bordeaux foncé. **5.** Maquillez bien les cils supérieurs avec un mascara en dirigeant les cils vers l'extérieur. Appliquez un rouge à lèvres de nuance rouge vif sur les lèvres. **6.** Après l'application du rouge à lèvres, tamponnez-les avec un kleenex. A la fin, ajoutez un peu de blush de teinte froide

DEUTSCH

1. Kaschieren Sie Problemzonen mit einem Concealer in einem natürlichen hellen Farbton. Eine mattierende Foundation verleiht Ihnen einen ebenmäßigen Teint. **2.** Verwenden Sie einen weichen, weißen Stift und heben Sie die Augenbrauenform von hinten an und lassen Sie das obere Augenlid so optisch voluminöser erscheinen. Betonen Sie den inneren Augenwinkel, das Kinn, begradigen Sie den Nasenrücken und heben Sie die Wangenknochen mit einem weißen matten Puder hervor. Betonen Sie die Nasenflügel mit einem dunklen Puder und tragen Sie dieses auf die Wangen und seitlichen Stirnpartien auf. **3.** Tragen Sie braune Lidschatten auf die obere Augenlidfalte und unteren Wimpernrand auf, um das Auge optisch zu verlängern und den Augenlidern mehr Volumen zu verleihen. Tragen Sie einen dunklen, braunen Lidschatten auf den Augenwinkel auf. Tragen Sie Rouge in einem natürlichen Farbton auf die Wangenknochen auf. **4.** Ziehen Sie die Augenbrauen mit einem schwarzen Stift nach und bringen Sie diese mit einem transparenten Gel in Form. Betonen Sie den äußeren Augenwinkel mit einem verwischten Pfeil entlang des oberen Augenlids. Ziehen Sie die Lippenkontur mit einem matten, kastanienbraunen Stift nach. **5.** Tragen Sie auf den oberen Wimperkranz Mascara auf und betonen Sie diesen stärker zum äußeren Außenwinkel hin. Verwenden Sie einen knallroten Lippenstift für die Lippen. **6.** Tupfen Sie die Lippen mit einem Tuch trocken und tragen Sie etwas Rouge in einem kühleren Farbton auf.

ESPAÑOL

1. Ocultar las áreas problemáticas de la piel con un corrector de un tono natural. Emparejar el tono y la textura de la piel con una base matizadora. **2.** Mediante un lápiz suave de color blanco, elevar visualmente la línea de las cejas, desde atrás, para darle más volumen al párpado superior. Resaltar el borde interior del ojo, afinar la pera, hacer más recto el arco de la nariz y marcar más claramente los pómulos con un polvo mate de color blanco. Acentuar las alas de la nariz con polvo más oscuro; oscurecer las mejillas y los laterales de la frente. **3.** Dibujar el pliegue del párpado superior y la línea inferior de las pestañas con sombra marrón alargando los ojos y haciendo que los párpados luzcan más voluminosos. Acentuar el borde del ojo con una sombra marrón oscura. Aplicar rubor de un tono natural en los pómulos. **4.** Dibujar las cejas con un lápiz negro y modelarlas con un gel translúcido para cejas. Acentuar el borde del ojo con una flecha difuminada sobre el párpado superior. Contornear los labios con lápiz mate de color granate. **5.** Pintar completamente las pestañas superiores con una máscara, dirigiéndolas hacia el borde externo del ojo. Utilizar lápiz labial rojo brillante para los labios. **6.** Secar los labios con un papel tissue. Agregar rubor de un tono frío.

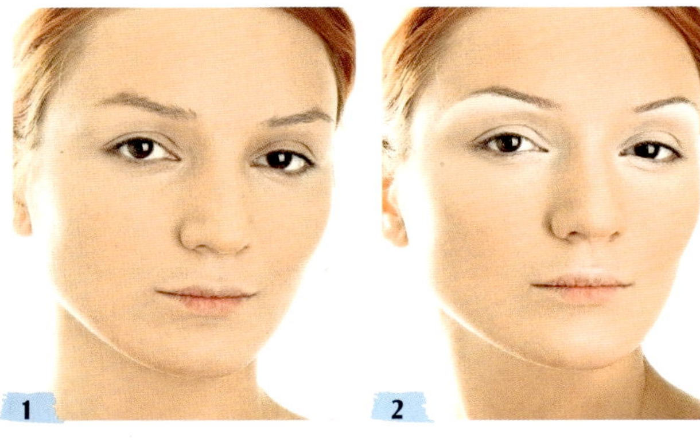

Model: Irina Kovalyova

AUDREY HEPBURN STYLE

ENGLISH

1. Mask problem skin areas with a concealer of a natural light shade. Even the tone and texture of the skin with mattifying foundation close to the skin tone. **2.** Using light beige shadow, lift the eyebrow line visually from behind and make the upper eyelid more voluminous with, highlighting the inner eye corner. Accentuate the nasal arch, forehead, cheekbones and chin with light powder. Using darker powder make the face more voluminous by darkening the temples, cheeks and alae of the nose. Accentuate the complexion with blusher of a natural shade. **3.** Using brown matte shadow, draw the upper eyelid crease, accentuate the lower eyelid and smudge the lines enlarging the eye visually. Accentuate the outer eye corner to "lift it up" visually. **4.** Accentuate the eyebrow shape with a brown pencil, style the eyebrow with translucent gel. **5.** Accentuate the upper eyelid with a black arrow line along the whole lash line. **6.** Color the eyelashes with lengthening mascara. Apply a matte lip color of a natural dark shade to the lips.

FRANÇAIS

1. Dissimulez les imperfections de la peau et les zones à problèmes avec un correcteur de teinte naturelle claire. Unifiez le teint et le relief de la peau avec un fond de teint matifiant d'une couleur proche de celle de la carnation. **2.** Remontez la ligne des sourcils en appliquant une ombre beige clair sur l'arcade sourcilière. Rendez la paupière supérieure plus bombée en éclaircissant le coin interne de l'œil. A l'aide d'une poudre claire soulignez l'arrête du nez, le front, les pommettes et le menton. Appliquez une poudre foncée sur les tempes, les joues et les ailes des narines pour faire ressortir davantage les traits du visage et ses dimensions. Pour rehausser l'éclat du visage, utilisez un blush de teinte naturelle. **3.** Soulignez le pli palpébral supérieur et la paupière inférieure avec une ombre brune mate. Ensuite estompez les lignes pour agrandir le regard. Une touche d'ombre dans le coin externe de l'œil permettra de le rehausser. **4.** Marquez le contour des sourcils avec un crayon brun, ensuite fixez-les avec un gel incolore. **5.** Dessinez un trait de liner le long des cils de la paupière supérieure pour l'accentuer. **6.** Mettez un mascara allongeant sur les cils. Pour les lèvres, utilisez un rouge à lèvres mat de teinte naturelle foncée.

DEUTSCH

1. Kaschieren Sie Unregelmäßigkeiten mit einem Concealer in einem natürlichen hellen Farbton. Tragen Sie eine mattierende Foundation, die Ihrem natürlichen Hautton entspricht auf, um einen ebenmäßigen Teint zu erhalten. **2.** Verwenden Sie einen hellen, beigefarbenen Lidschatten und heben Sie die Augenbrauen optisch von hinten an und verleihen Sie dem oberen Augenlid durch Betonung des inneren Augenwinkels mehr Volumen. Betonen Sie den Nasenrücken, die Stirn, die Wangenknochen und das Kinn mit einem hellen Puder. Durch Auftragen eines dunkleren Puders auf die Schläfen, Wangen und Nasenflügel verleihen Sie dem Gesicht mehr Volumen. Tragen Sie zum Abschluss ein natürliches Rouge auf. **3.** Tragen Sie einen matten, braunen Lidschatten auf die obere Augenlidfalte auf, betonen Sie das untere Augenlid und verwischen Sie die Linien, um das Auge optisch zu verlängern. Betonen Sie den äußeren Augenwinkel, um das Auge optisch „anzuheben".
4. Betonen Sie die Augenbrauenform mit einem braunen Stift und bringen Sie diese mit einem transparenten Gel in Form. **5.** Betonen Sie das obere Augenlid mit einer schwarzen Pfeillinie entlang des gesamten Wimpernrands. **6.** Tragen Sie wimpernverlängernde Mascara auf. Vervollständigen Sie den Look mit einem matten Lippenstift in einem natürlichen dunklen Farbton.

ESPAÑOL

1. Ocultar las áreas problemáticas de la piel con un corrector de color natural claro. Emparejar el tono y la textura de la piel con una base matizadora de un color similar al de la piel. **2.** Utilizando una sombra de color beige claro, realzar el borde interior del ojo elevando visualmente la línea de las cejas, desde atrás, para hacer más voluminoso el párpado superior. Acentuar el arco de la nariz, la frente, los pómulos y la pera, con polvo claro. Oscurecer las sienes, las mejillas y las alas de la nariz utilizando polvo más oscuro para dar más volumen a la cara. Acentuar el rostro con un rubor de un tono natural.
3. Mediante una sombra mate de color marrón dibujar el pliegue del párpado superior, realzando el borde exterior del ojo para elevarlo visualmente. **4.** Realzar la forma de las cejas con un lápiz marrón, modelarlas con un gel translúcido. **5.** Acentuar el párpado superior con una línea, todo a lo largo de la línea de las pestañas. **6.** Pintar las pestañas con una máscara alargadora. Aplicar un labial mate de un color natural oscuro a los labios.

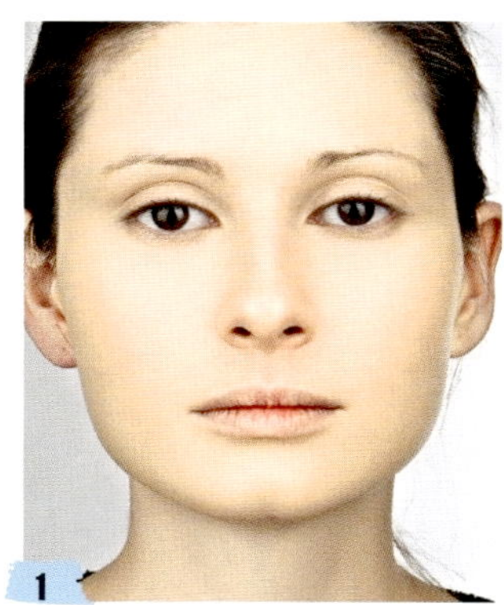
1

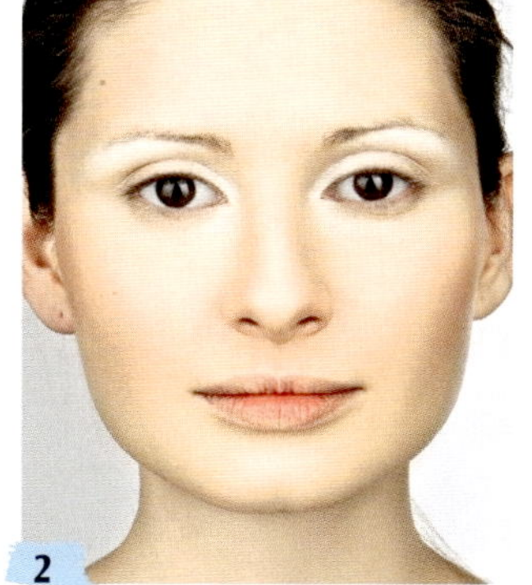
2

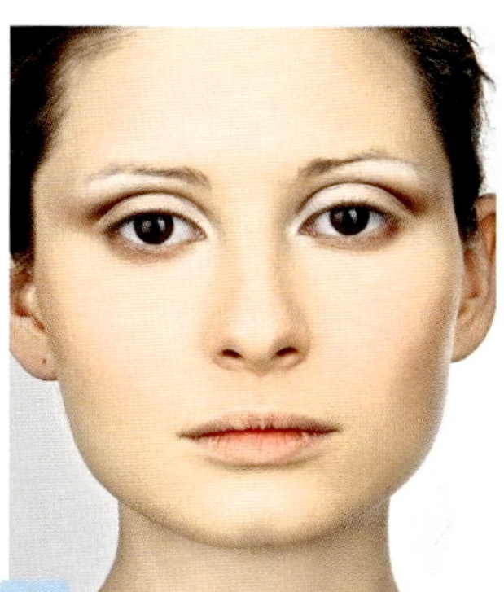
3

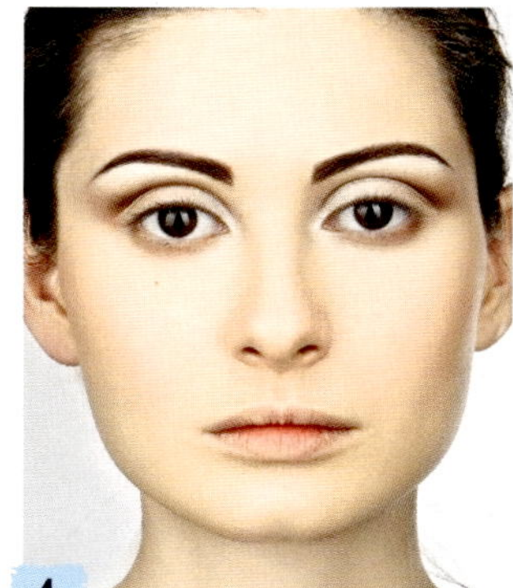
4

5

6

Model: Olga Cherkes

MARILYN MONROE STYLE

ENGLISH

Even the skin tone with mattifying foundation. **2.** Using a light concealer even the nasal arch, correct the shape of the cheekbones and chin. Apply white matte shadow to the inner eye corner and upper movable lid; apply the same shadow to the area under the eyebrow. **3.** Finish the correction with dark powder. Apply it to the alae of the nose, cheeks and lateral parts of the forehead. **4.** Draw a line with brown matte shadow a little above the upper eyelid crease. Smudge the line towards the eyebrow to create a false eyebrow line. Accentuate the outer corner of the lower eyelid with the same shadow. **5.** Accentuate the eyebrows with a taupe pencil making them more "graphic". Apply beige blusher with satin shine to the cheekbones. **6.** Draw neat "arrows" along the whole upper eyelash line with a liquid eyeliner. To make the image look like Marilyn Monroe even more, glue angles of false lashes to both upper and lower eyelids. This will make the look languish. **7.** Color the eyelashes with black mascara. **8.** To contour the lips use a pencil of a maroon shade. Contour the lips rounding up their shape visually. Apply rich red lip color over the pencil. As a finishing touch, draw a small beauty small with a brown pencil.

FRANÇAIS

1. Unifiez le teint du visage avec un fond de teint matifiant. **2.** A l'aide d'un correcteur clair redressez l'arête du nez, corrigez la forme des pommettes et du menton. Appliquez une ombre blanche mate dans sur l'arcade sourcilière, arrondissez la paupière supérieure. **3.** Pour terminer la correction du visage, utilisez une poudre foncée : soulignez les ailes des narines, balayez les joues et les côtés du front. **4.** Dessinez une ligne légèrement au-dessus du pli palpébral supérieur avec une ombre brune mate. Estompez la ligne en la ramenant vers les sourcils pour donner une impression de profondeur et faire ainsi remonter la limite de la paupière. Soulignez le coin externe de la paupière inférieure avec la même ombre. **5.** Dessinez le contour des sourcils avec un crayon gris-brun en les rendant plus graphiques et anguleux. Appliquez un fard à joues aux reflets satinés de teinte beige sur les pommettes. **6.** Tracez soigneusement un trait avec un eye-liner fluide noir au ras des cils sur toute la paupière supérieure. Collez des morceaux de faux cils sur les paupières supérieure et inférieure. **7.** Mettez un mascara noir sur les cils. **8.** Dessiner le contour des lèvres avec un crayon à lèvres de nuance rouge foncé. Remplissez les lèvres avec un rouge à lèvres de couleur rouge profond. Dessinez une petite « mouche » sur la joue avec un crayon brun foncé.

DEUTSCH

1. Tragen Sie eine mattierende Foundation auf, um einen ebenmäßigen Teint zu erhalten. **2.** Korrigieren Sie den Nasenrücken, die Form der Wangenknochen und des Kinns mit einem hellen Concealer. Tragen Sie einen matten, weißen Lidschatten auf den inneren Augenwinkel, das obere bewegliche Augenlid und den Bereich unterhalb der Augenbrauen auf. **3.** Verwenden Sie zum Abschluss einen dunklen Puder und tragen diesen auf Nasenflügel, Wangen und seitlichen Stirnpartien auf. **4.** Tragen Sie einen matten, braunen Lidschatten auf die obere Augenlidfalte auf. Verwischen Sie die Linien zur Augenbraue hin, um eine falsche Augenbrauenlinie zu kreieren. Betonen Sie den äußeren Augenwinkel des unteren Augenlids mit der gleichen Lidschattenfarbe. **5.** Betonen Sie die Augenbrauen mit einem graubraunen Stift, um diese „grafischer" zu gestalten. Tragen Sie ein beigefarbenes Rouge mit Satinglanz auf die Wangenknochen auf. **6.** Malen Sie mit einem flüssigen Eyeliner deutliche „Pfeile" entlang des oberen Wimpernrands. Kleben Sie auf den oberen und unteren Wimpernrand künstliche Wimpern auf, um einen Marilyn-Monroe-Look zu erhalten. So verleihen Sie Ihren Augen einen schmachtenden Blick. **7.** Tragen Sie schwarze Mascara auf. **8.** Ziehen Sie die Lippenkontur mit einem kastanienbraunen Lipliner nach und verleihen diesen eine optisch rundere Form. Tragen Sie einen tiefroten Lippenstift auf. Malen Sie mit einem braunen Stift ein kleines Muttermal auf, um den Look zu vervollständigen.

ESPAÑOL

1. Emparejar el tono de la piel con una base matizadora. **2.** Con un corrector claro emparejar el arco de la nariz, corregir la forma de los pómulos y la pera. Aplicar una sombra blanca mate en el borde interior del ojo y en el párpado móvil superior, aplicar la misma sombra al área bajo las cejas. **3.** Finalizar las correcciones con polvo más oscuro. Aplicarlo a las alas de la nariz, a las mejillas y a los laterales de la frente. **4.** Trazar una línea con una sombra mate de color marrón apenas arriba del pliegue del párpado superior. Esfumar la línea hacia la ceja para crear una falsa línea de ceja. Realzar el borde externo del párpado inferior con la misma sombra. **5.** Realzar las cejas con un lápiz de color topo para hacerlas más "diseñadas". Aplicar un rubor beige con brillo satinado en los pómulos. **6.** Trazar una flecha todo a lo largo de la línea de las pestañas superiores con un delineador líquido. Para lograr una imagen más parecida aún a Marilyn Monroe, adherir pestañas postizas azules en el ángulo de las pestañas superiores e inferiores. Así se logrará una mirada lánguida. **7.** Pintar las pestañas con máscara negra. **8.** Para contornear los labios usar un lápiz de un tono granate. Contornearlos redondeando visualmente su forma. Aplicar un labial de color rojo intenso sobre el lápiz. Como toque final, dibujar un pequeño lunar con un lápiz marrón.

1

2

3

4

5

6

7

8

Model: Maria Litovchenko

TWIGGY STYLE

ENGLISH

1. Mask problem skin areas with a concealer of a natural light shade. Even the tone and texture of the skin with mattifying foundation. **2.** Using a white soft pencil, lift the eyebrow line visually from behind and make the upper eyelid more voluminous, highlight the inner eye corner. Using white matte powder, sharpen the chin, highlight the nasal arch accentuating the end, and make the cheekbone line softer. **3.** Accentuate the alae of the nose slightly lengthening it. Darken the cheeks and lateral parts of the forehead to make it higher visually. Draw a false upper eyelid crease with light brown shadow a little higher the real one. Accentuate the lower eyelid in the same way, rounding it up. **4.** Draw a raised crease of the upper eyelid with a dark brown pencil, smudging the crease upwards and lowering it towards the outer eye corner in a grotesque way. Change the eyebrow shape with a brown pencil. **5.** Style the eyebrows with translucent gel more neatly accentuating their new shape. Draw an arrow line along the whole upper eyelid accentuating the lowered outer eye corner. Draw a thin arrow along the whole lower eyelid, starting from it draw grotesque eyelashes making them larger towards the outer eye corner. Accentuate the lower eyelash line with a white eyeliner. **6.** To make the look more open, use false eyelashes. Apply gloss of a natural shade to the lips.

FRANÇAIS

1. Dissimulez les imperfections de la peau avec un correcteur de teinte naturelle claire. Unifiez le teint et le relief de la peau avec un fond de teint matifiant. **2.** Relevez la ligne des sourcils en appliquant un crayon gras blanc sur l'arcade sourcilière, rendez la paupière mobile supérieure plus apparente en éclaircissant le coin interne de l'œil. Avec une poudre blanche mate, sculptez la forme du menton pour le rendre plus allongé, éclaircissez l'arête du nez en accentuant la pointe du nez et adoucissez la ligne des pommettes. **3.** Avec une poudre foncée, soulignez les ailes des narines pour rendre le nez plus long. Foncez les joues et les côtés du front pour le rendre visuellement plus haut. Dessinez la ligne du pli palpébral légèrement au-dessus de sa ligne naturelle avec une ombre gris-brun. Soulignez la paupière inférieure avec la même ombre pour l'arrondir. **4.** Repassez un crayon brun foncé sur la ligne au-dessus du pli palpébral d'origine. Estompez la ligne en l'étalant vers le haut. Finalisez la ligne dessinée en l'étirant vers le bas avec exagération. Changez la forme des sourcils en utilisant un crayon brun. **5.** Arrangez les sourcils avec un gel incolore, soulignez leur nouvelle forme. Redessinez la totalité de la ligne supérieure des cils avec un eye-liner fluide en mettant accent « tombant » sur les coins des yeux. Le long des cils inférieurs tracez un trait fin, dessinez des cils « grotesques » en les rendant plus longs vers l'extérieur de l'œil. Marquez le contour de la paupière inférieure, le long de la racine des cils, avec un trait de crayon blanc. **6.** Pour un regard extra large, utilisez des faux cils. Appliquez un gloss de nuance naturelle sur les lèvres.

DEUTSCH

1. Kaschieren Sie Unregelmäßigkeiten mit einem Concealer in einem natürlichen, hellen Ton. Eine mattierende Foundation in einem Ihrem Hautton entsprechenden Farbton. **2.** Verwenden Sie einen weißen, weichen Stift und heben Sie die Augenbraue optisch von hinten an und betonen Sie den inneren Augenwinkel, um das Augenlid voluminöser erscheinen zu lassen. Verwenden Sie einen matten, weißen Puder, betonen Sie das Kinn, den Nasenrücken, die Nasenspitze und gestalten Sie die Wangenknochen weicher. **3.** Betonen Sie die Nasenflügel, um die Nase somit leicht zu verlängern. Verdunkeln Sie die Wangen und seitlichen Stirnpartien etwas, um diese optisch zu erhöhen. Tragen Sie mit einem hellbraunen Lidschatten eine falsche Augenlidfalte am oberen Lid, etwas höher als die eigentliche Lidfalte, auf. Betonen Sie das untere Augenlid ebenso. **4.** Gestalten Sie mit einem dunkelbraunen Stift eine erhöhte obere Augenlidfalte und lassen Sie den Strich zum äußeren Augenwinkel hin auf eine fast groteske Weise nach unten abfallen. Ändern Sie die natürliche Augenbrauenform mit einem braunen Stift. **5.** Bringen Sie die Augenbrauen mit einem transparenten Gel in die neue Form. Ziehen Sie eine Pfeillinie entlang des oberen Augenlids, um den tiefer gesetzten äußeren Augenwinkel zu betonen. Ziehen Sie einen dünnen Pfeil entlang des gesamten unteren Augenlids und malen Sie groteske Wimpern auf, die zum äußeren Augenwinkel hin länger werden. Betonen Sie den unteren Wimpernrand mit einem weißen Eyeliner. **6.** Verwenden Sie falsche Wimpern, um einen offenen Blick zu erhalten. Tragen Sie ein natürliches Lipgloss auf.

ESPAÑOL

1. Ocultar las áreas problemáticas de la piel con un corrector de un tono natural claro. Emparejar el tono y la textura de la piel con una base matizadora. **2.** Utilizando un lápiz suave de color blanco, elevar visualmente la línea de las cejas, desde atrás, y lograr un párpado superior más voluminoso, resaltar el borde interior del ojo. Utilizando un polvo mate de color blanco, afilar la pera, destacar el arco de la nariz acentuando la punta y hacer la línea del pómulo más suave. **3.** Realzar las alas de la nariz para alargarla apenas. Oscurecer las mejillas y los laterales de la frente para que luzca más alta. Dibujar un falso pliegue en el párpado superior, un poco más alto que el real, con una sombra marrón clara. Realzar el párpado inferior del mismo modo. Redondeándolo. **4.** Dibujar un pliegue elevado del párpado superior con un lápiz marrón, esfumando el pliegue hacia arriba y bajándolo hacia el borde externo del ojo, de manera grotesca. Modificar la forma de las cejas con un lápiz marrón. **5.** Modelar las cejas con un gel translúcido acentuando la nueva forma. Dibujar una línea todo a lo largo del párpado superior, acentuando el borde externo inferior del ojo. Dibujar un línea angosta todo a lo largo del párpado inferior, desde esta línea trazar pestañas **6.** Para una mirada más abierta, utilice pestañas postizas. Aplique un brillo de color natural sobre los labios.

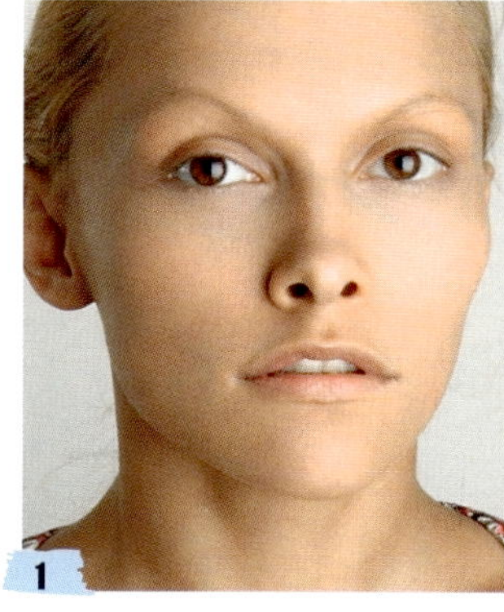
1

2

3

4

5

6

Model: Elya Brusnichkina

BARBRA STREISAND STYLE

ENGLISH

1. Even the tone and texture of the skin with mattifying foundation. **2.** Lift the eyebrow line visually from behind with light beige matte shadow. Using light powder, accentuate the nasal arch, forehead, cheekbones and chin. Make the face more voluminous with darker powder darkening the temples, cheeks, alae of the nose.
3. Accentuate the eyebrows with a dark brown pencil, style them with translucent gel. Draw the upper eyelid crease with beige matte shadow accentuating the outer corner, and smudge it extending the eye visually. **4.** Using dark brown shadow, draw the upper eyelid crease, accentuate the lower eyelid along all the lash line laying an emphasis upon the smudged arrow line. **5.** Accentuate the upper eyelid with a black arrow along the lash line. Using black shadow, connect the arrow line with the upper eyelid crease line. **6.** Apply light golden lip color to the lips. Color the eyelashes with lengthening mascara.

FRANÇAIS

1. Unifiez le teint et le relief de la peau avec un fond de teint matifiant. **2.** Remontez visuellement la ligne des sourcils en appliquant une ombre mate de teinte beige clair sur l'arcade sourcilière. Rendez la paupière supérieure plus bombée en éclaircissant le coin interne de l'œil. A l'aide d'une poudre claire soulignez l'arrête du nez, le front, les pommettes et le menton. Appliquez une poudre foncée sur les parties latérales du front, les joues et les ailes des narines pour faire ressortir davantage les traits du visage. **3.** Marquez le contour des sourcils avec un crayon brun foncé, ensuite « coiffez-les » à l'aide d'un gel incolore. Déposez une ombre beige mate dans le pli palpébral supérieur en accentuant l'angle externe. Ensuite ramenez vers l'extérieur de l'œil en estompant pour l'allonger visuellement. **4.** Recouvrez l'ombre beige qui marque le pli palpébral avec une ombre brun foncé. Laissez une trace au ras des cils de la paupière inférieure avec cette ombre en mettant l'accent sur l'extrémité extérieure du trait estompé. **5.** Soulignez la paupière supérieure avec un trait d'eye-liner noir au ras des cils. Reliez le trait d'eye-liner avec la ligne du pli palpébral à l'aide d'une ombre noire. **6.** Maquillez les lèvres avec un rouge à lèvres de teinte clair doré. Mettez un mascara allongeant sur les cils.

DEUTSCH

1. Eine mattierende Foundation verleiht Ihnen einen ebenmäßigen Teint. **2.** Heben Sie die Augenbrauen mit einem hellen, beigefarbenen, matten Lidschatten von hinten optisch an. Betonen Sie mit einem hellen Puder den Nasenrücken, die Stirn, Wangenknochen und das Kinn. Tragen Sie einen dunkleren Puder auf die Schläfen, Wangen und Nasenflügel auf, um dem Gesicht mehr Volumen zu verleihen. **3.** Betonen Sie die Augenbrauen mit einem dunkelbraunen Stift und bringen Sie diese mit transparentem Gel in Form. Ziehen Sie die obere Augenlidfalte mit einem matten beigefarbenen Lidschatten nach und betonen Sie den äußeren Winkel. Verwischen Sie diese, um das Auge optisch zu verlängern. **4.** Tragen Sie einen dunkelbraunen Lidschatten auf die obere Augenlidfalte auf, betonen Sie das untere Augenlid entlang des Wimpernrands und somit die verwischte Pfeillinie. **5.** Betonen Sie das obere Augenlid mit einem schwarzen Pfeil entlang des Wimpernrands. Verwenden Sie schwarzen Lidschatten, um die Pfeillinie mit der unteren Augenlidfalte zu verbinden. **6.** Tragen Sie einen hellen goldfarbenen Lippenstift auf die Lippen und eine wimpernverlängernde Mascara auf die Wimpern auf.

ESPAÑOL

1. Emparejar el tono y la textura de la piel con una base matizadora. **2.** Elevar visualmente la línea de la ceja, desde atrás, con una sombra mate de color beige claro. Con un polvo claro, realzar el arco de la nariz, la frente, los pómulos y la pera. Utilizar un polvo más oscuro en las sienes, las mejillas y las alas de la nariz para dar más volumen a la cara. **3.** Realzar las cejas con un lápiz marrón oscuro, modelarlas con un gel translúcido. Dibujar el pliegue del párpado superior con una sombra mate de color beige acentuando el borde externo y esfumándola, así se alargará, visualmente, el ojo. **4.** Utilizando una sombra marrón oscura, dibujar el pliegue del párpado superior, realzar el párpado inferior todo a lo largo de la línea de pestañas, enfatizando la línea esfumada. **5.** Realzar el párpado superior con una flecha negra a lo largo de la línea de pestañas. Utilizando una sombra negra conectar la flecha con la línea del pliegue del párpado superior. **6.** Aplicar un labial de color dorado claro sobre los labios. Pintar las pestañas con una máscara alargadora.

1

2

3

4

5

6

Model: Ekaterina Chistova

MADONNA STYLE

ENGLISH

1. Mask problem skin areas with a concealer of a natural light shade. Even the tone and texture of the skin with mattifying foundation close to the skin tone. **2.** Using a white soft pencil, lift the eyebrow line visually from behind, make the upper movable lid more voluminous highlighting the inner eye corner. Make the chin sharper, straighten the nasal arch and make the cheekbone line clearer with white matte powder. **3.** Accentuate the alae of the nose with dark making the straight line of the nasal arch clearer. Darken the cheeks and lateral parts of the forehead. Draw the upper eyeline crease and lower lash line with light brown shadow extending the eye and making the eyelid more voluminous. **4.** Accentuate the eye corner with dark brown shadow extending it with a smudged arrow line from above and behind. Change the eyebrow shape with a brown pencil. Contour the lips with a red matte pencil. **5.** Style the eyebrows with translucent gel more neatly accentuating their new shape. Color the lower lashes slightly, the upper ones – more intensively, setting the direction towards the outer eye corner. Apply a bright red lipstick to the lips. **6.** Blot the lips with a dry tissue. Add a little blusher of a natural shade.

FRANÇAIS

1. Dissimulez les zones à problèmes avec un correcteur de teinte naturelle claire. Unifiez le teint et le relief de la peau avec un fond de teint matifiant de couleur proche à la carnation de la peau. **2.** Remontez visuellement la ligne des sourcils en appliquant une ombre mate de teinte beige clair sur l'arcade sourcilière. Rendez la paupière supérieure plus bombée en éclaircissant le coin interne de l'œil. A l'aide d'une poudre claire rendez le menton plus allongé, la ligne des pommettes plus prononcée, redressez l'arrête du nez. **3.** Appliquez une poudre foncée sur les ailes des narines pour accentuer davantage la ligne droite de l'arrête du nez. Foncez les joues et les côtés du front. Déposez une ombre brun clair dans le pli palpébral et soulignez la ligne de la paupière inférieure pour allonger visuellement l'œil et apporter du volume à la paupière. **4.** Rehaussez l'angle externe de l'œil en traçant des traits sur le haut et sur le bas de l'œil en les estompant et étirant vers l'extérieur de l'œil avec une ombre brun foncé. Cela permettra d'allonger les yeux. Changez la forme des sourcils à l'aide d'un crayon brun. Pour les lèvres, utilisez un crayon à lèvres mat rouge. **5.** « Coiffez » les sourcils soigneusement à l'aide d'un gel incolore en renforçant la forme obtenue grâce au crayon. Maquillez légèrement les cils du bas, appliquez plus de mascara sur ceux du haut en les dirigeant vers le coin externe de l'œil. Mettez un rouge à lèvres de teinte rouge vif. **6.** Après l'application du rouge à lèvres, tamponnez-les avec un kleenex. A la fin, saupoudrer le visage d'un peu de blush de teinte naturelle.

DEUTSCH

1. Kaschieren Sie Unregelmäßigkeiten mit einem Concealer in einem natürlichen Farbton. Eine mattierende Foundation verleiht Ihnen einen ebenmäßigen Teint. **2.** Verwenden Sie einen weißen, weichen Stift, um die Augenbraue optisch von hinten anzuheben. Durch Betonung des inneren Augenwinkels erscheint das obere bewegliche Augenlid voluminöser. Betonen Sie das Kinn, begradigen Sie den Nasenrücken und heben Sie die Wangenknochen mit einem matten, weißen Puder hervor. **3.** Betonen Sie die Nasenflügel mit einem dunkleren Farbton, um den geraden Nasenrücken hervorzuheben. Tragen Sie den gleichen Farbton auch auf die Wangen und seitlichen Stirnpartien auf. Ziehen Sie die obere Augenlidfalte und den unteren Wimpernrand mit einem hellbraunen Lidschatten nach, um das Auge optisch zu verlängern und somit zu vergrößern. **4.** Betonen Sie den Augenwinkel mit einem dunkelbraunen Lidschatten und erweitern Sie diesen mit einer verwischen Pfeillinie von oben und hinten. Verändern Sie die Augenbrauenform mit einem braunen Stift. Ziehen Sie die Lippenkonturen mit einem matten roten Lipliner nach. **5.** Bringen Sie die Augenbrauen mit einem transparenten Gel in ihre neue Form. Tragen Sie dezent Mascara auf die unteren Wimpern auf. Betonen Sie die oberen Wimpern stärker zum äußeren Augenwinkel hin. Tragen Sie einen knallroten Lippenstift auf. **6.** Tupfen Sie die Lippen mit einem trockenen Tuch ab. Tragen Sie etwas Rouge in einem natürlichen Farbton auf.

ESPAÑOL

1. Ocultar las áreas problemáticas de la piel con un corrector de un tono natural claro. Emparejar el tono y la textura de la piel con una base matizadora de un tono similar al de la piel. **2.** Utilizando un lápiz suave de color blanco, elevar visualmente la línea de las cejas, desde atrás. Resaltar el borde interior del ojo para dar más volumen al párpado superior móvil. Afilar la pera, enderezar el arco de la nariz y hacer que la línea de los pómulos sea más clara con un polvo mate blanco. **3.** Oscurecer las alas de la nariz haciendo que la línea recta del arco de la nariz sea más clara. Oscurecer las mejillas y los laterales de la frente. Dibujar la línea del pliegue del párpado superior y la línea de las pestañas inferiores con una sombra marrón, alargando el ojo y dando más volumen al párpado. **4.** Realzar el borde del ojo con sombra marrón oscura alargándola con una línea difuminada desde abajo y atrás. Modificar la forma de las cejas con un lápiz marrón. Contornear los labios con un lápiz mate de color rojo. **5.** Modelar las cejas con un gel translúcido, más nítidamente, acentuando la nueva forma. Pintar apenas las pestañas inferiores y las superiores más intensamente, dirigiéndolas hacia el borde externo del ojo. Aplicar un lápiz labial rojo sobre los labios. **6.** Secar los labios con un papel tissue. Agregar apenas rubor de un tono natural.

1

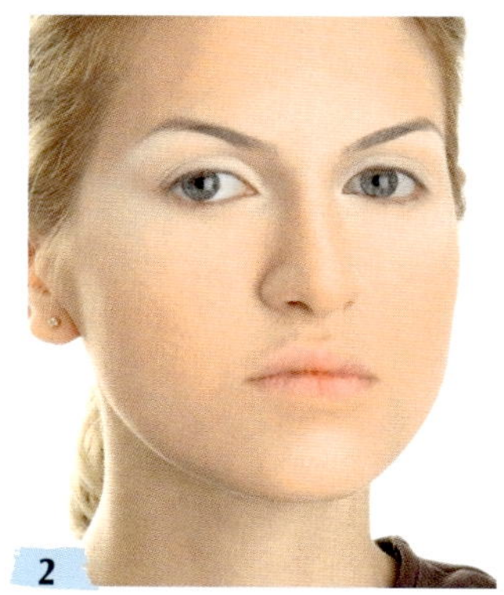
2

3

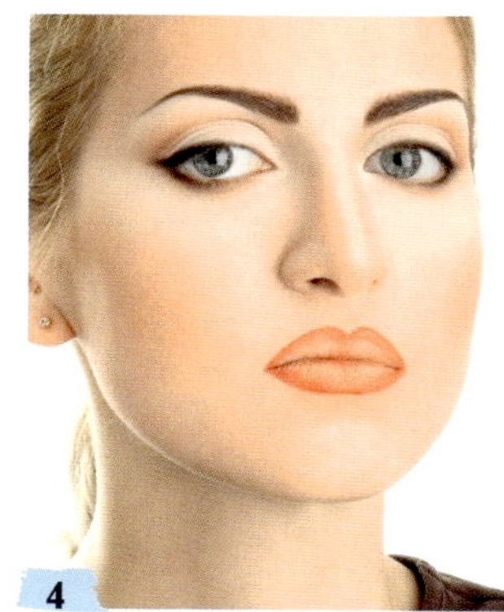
4

5

6

Model: Elena Kostina

WHITNEY HOUSTON STYLE

ENGLISH

1. Mask problem skin areas with a concealer a shade lighter than the skin tone. Even the skin tone using a foundation with a matte effect.
2. Using a light matte powder, sharpen the chin, accentuate the bridge of the nose, make the cheekbone line more defined, and lighten the central part of the forehead to make it higher.
3. Emphasize the alae of the nose with dark powder. Darken the cheeks and lateral parts of the forehead.
4. Draw the upper lid and upper and lower eyelash line with a black pencil, lengthening the eye and lifting its outer corner. Correct the eyebrow shape using a light compact concealer and brown pencil. Style the eyebrows with transparent gel. **5.** Accentuate the outer eye corner with green pearl shadow. Apply light pearl shadow below the eyebrow and the upper lid. **6.** Brighten the look by applying a little rouge to the cheekbones and upper lid. Color the eyelashes, moving towards the outer eye corner. Apply a saturated plum color lipstick to the lips.

FRANÇAIS

1. Camouflez les zones à problèmes avec un correcteur de teinte naturelle claire. Unifiez le teint et le relief de la peau avec un fond de teint matifiant. **2.** Avec une poudre mate claire affinez le menton, redressez l'arête du nez, rendez la ligne des pommettes plus prononcée, et éclaircissez le centre du front, en le rendant plus haut. **3.** Avec une poudre foncée, accentuez les ailes du nez. Foncez les joues et les parties latérales du front. **4.** Tracez un trait sur le pli palpébral supérieur et sur la ligne des cils supérieurs et inférieurs avec un crayon noir, afin d'allonger la forme des yeux et de relever le coin externe de l'œil. Avec un correcteur clair à texture dense et un crayon brun, corrigez la forme des sourcils. Appliquez un gel incolore sur les sourcils.
5. Estompez le crayon noir avec des ombres vertes à l'effet nacré, en mettant l'accent sur le coin externe de l'œil. Pour obtenir plus de volume ajoutez du nacre clair sous les sourcils et sur la paupière mobile supérieure. **6.** Appliquez un peu de fards à joues de ton froid sur les pommettes et la paupière supérieure pour « revivifier » le maquillage. Maquillez les cils, en les dirigeant vers le coin externe de l'œil. Appliquez sur les lèvres un rouge à lèvres de ton prune vif.

DEUTSCH

1. Kaschieren Sie Problemzonen mit einem Concealer, der eine Nuance heller ist, als Ihr Hautton. Verwenden Sie eine matte Foundation, um einen ebenmäßigen Teint zu erhalten.
2. Tragen Sie ein helles mattes Puder auf, um das Kinn und den Nasenrücken zu betonen. Betonen Sie die Wangenknochen und den mittleren Stirnbereich, um diese höher erscheinen zu lassen. **3.** Betonen Sie den Nasenrücken, Wangen und seitlichen Stirnpartien mit dunklem Puder.
4. Ziehen Sie das obere und untere Augenlid sowie den unteren Wimpernrand mit einem schwarzen Kajal nach, um das Auge optisch zu strecken und die äußeren Winkel anzuheben. Korrigieren Sie die Augenbrauenform mit einem hellen Kompakt-Concealer und einem braunem Augenbrauenstift. Bringen Sie die Augenbrauen mit einem transparenten Augenbrauengel in Form.
5. Betonen Sie den äußeren Augenwinkel mit einem grünen perlmuttfarbigen Lidschatten. Tragen Sie einen hellen Perlmutt-Lidschatten unterhalb der Augenbraue und auf dem oberen Augenlid auf. **6.** Frischen Sie den Look mit einem hellen Rouge, durch Auftragen auf die Wangenknochen und das obere Augenlid auf. Tragen Sie Mascara zum äußeren Augenwinkel hin auf. Vervollständigen Sie den Look mit einem satten pflaumenfarbenen Lippenstift.

ESPAÑOL

1. Ocultar las áreas problemáticas de la piel con un corrector un tono más claro que el de la piel. Emparejar el tono de la piel usando una base con un efecto mate. **2.** Utilizando un polvo mate claro, afilar la pera, realzar el puente de la nariz, hacer que la línea de los pómulos sea más definida y, aligerar la parte central de la frente para que luzca más alta.
3. Enfatizar las alas de la nariz con polvo oscuro. Oscurecer las mejillas y las partes laterales de la frente.
4. Dibujar el párpado superior y la línea de las pestañas inferiores y superiores con un lápiz negro, alargando el ojo y elevando su borde externo. Corregir la forma de las cejas utilizando un corrector compacto claro y un lápiz marrón. Modelar las cejas con un gel transparente.
5. Realzar el borde externo de los ojos con una sombra perlada de color verde. Aplicar sombra perlada clara debajo de las cejas y en el párpado superior. **6.** Para destacar aplicar rojo en los pómulos y en el párpado superior. Pintar las pestañas dirigiéndolas hacia el borde externo del ojo. Aplicar un lápiz labial de un color ciruela saturado sobre los labios.

1

2

3

4

5

6

Model: Liliya Nyemenim

Volume 17 / Volumen 17/ Volume 17/ Band 17

MAKE UP

Published by / Publicado por / Publié par/ Herausgegeben von

HAIR'S HOW
5645 Coral Ridge Drive # 131
Coral Springs, FL 33076, USA
Ph. 1-954-323-8590, Fax 1-951-344-2240
e-mail: publisher@hairshow.us

Distributed by / Distribuido por / Distribué par/ Vertrieben von

HAIR'S HOW
5645 Coral Ridge Drive # 131
Coral Springs, FL 33076, USA
Ph. 1-954-323-8590, Fax 1-951-344-2240
www.hairshow.us, e-mail: sales@hairshow.us

HAIR'S HOW, VOLUME 17: MAKE UP
HAIR'S HOW, VOLUME 17: MAKE UP
HAIR'S HOW, VOLUME 17 : MAKE UP
HAIR'S HOW, BAND 17: MAKE UP

ISBN 978-0-98467353-7

Printed in EU / Impreso en EU / Imprimé en Europe/Gedruckt in der EU

First edition / Primera edición / Première edition/ Erste Auflage